PLAIN LIVING

# PLAIN LIVING

A QUAKER PATH TO SIMPLICITY

WITH A FOREWORD BY PARKER PALMER

CATHERINE WHITMIRE

SORIN BOOKS   Notre Dame, IN

CATHERINE WHITMIRE has held several leadership roles in her community, including supervising empowerment projects in New England and working as an Alternatives to Violence trainer in various jails and prisons. A Quaker for twenty-five years, she holds a Master of Divinity from Harvard Divinity School and has served as a chaplain and hospital pastoral counselor. She currently resides in Maine and continues her writing and speaking engagements on the East Coast.

Copyright acknowledgments may be found on page 189.

www.sorinbooks.com

International Standard Book Number: 1-893732-28-2

Cover design by Angela Moody, Moving Images

Cover photo: *Field* © 2000, Christopher Diers

Text design by Katherine Robinson Coleman

Printed and bound in the United States of America.

*Library of Congress Cataloging-in-Publication Data*
Whitmire, Catherine.
Plain living : a Quaker path to simplicity / Catherine Whitmire.
    p. cm.
    ISBN 1-893732-28-2 (pbk.)
1. Simplicity--Religious aspects--Christianity. 2. Spiritual life--Society of Friends. I. Title.
BV4647.S48 W48 2001
248.4'896--dc21

2001002441
CIP

*For Zachary*

*and the next generation*

*and*

*In gratitude to*

*Friends Meeting at Cambridge*

# Contents

I am deeply grateful to the Religious Society of Friends for their testimony on plain living, and for the many Friends living and dead whose wisdom and witness contribute to the writing of this book.

This compilation of quotations would not have been possible without the inter-library loan desk at the Cape Elizabeth Library, the Andover Library at Harvard, and the Haverford College Quaker Collection whose hospitality and helpfulness are deeply appreciated.

Parts of this book have been written on retreat and nurtured by the rolling surf at Eastern Point Retreat House, the cry of the wolf at Ring Lake Ranch, the quiet solitude of the Transfiguration Hermitage, the inspiration of the Shalem Institute, and the joyous singing of the brothers at Weston Priory.

From Portland Friends Meeting, Mary Hillis, Barbara Potter, and Susan Marks held me in prayer. Phil and Gail Davis and Pam and Scott Wessel-Estes offered continuous long-distance support and encouragement. Bob Brizee helped me begin my journey. Joe and Mary Roy believed in my first leading. Carol Becker encouraged me to trust my heart.

My thanks to Penny Yunuba, Mary Hillis, Barbara Potter, Gwendolyn Noyes, Tim and Mary Ann Nicholson, Ed Snyder, Molly Gregory, and many others who were generous with their time and gracious in their willingness to share their stories.

I am appreciative of those whose varied perspectives helped me discern particular aspects of the text: Robin Gradison, Cynthia Maciel Knowles, Benjamin Snyder, Joanna Pool, Charlotte Fardleman, and Beth Bussiere. Katy Cullinan graciously shared her editorial gifts. Sirkka and Hugh Barbour offered hospitality and loaned books, and Hugh's witty and wise historical perspectives deepened the text. Jonathan Ewell was a perceptive editor and his vision, reflective of the new generation, lightened the draft. I am grateful to John Kirvan at Sorin Books for initiating the invitation to write this book and to Julie Hahnenberg who edited the final manuscript with gentle patience and attention to detail.

I feel a special debt of gratitude to my Quaker writers' group for the encouragement and feedback I needed to persevere. Beckey Phipps offered hospitality and warm encouragement. Janet Hoffman offered not only incisive comments but searched her files for articles, shared her journal, and sent books that arrived in manila envelopes with colored stickers on the days I most needed to receive them. Margaret Benefiel listened the first drafts into being, encouraged me, and prayed for the book from the beginning.

I am thankful for my soul-friend, Barbara Cummings St. John, whose friendship makes the world a warmer place and whose wisdom and stories illumine these pages. I am also thankful for my dear Spirit-Friend, Emily Sander, who read every draft, whose love I count among my greatest blessings, and whose wisdom gave me a deeper appreciation and understanding of plain living.

I am thankful for the ongoing friendship of Sharon Daloz Parks—the Spirit speaks through her life. Through her I began graduate school, met my husband, and came to write this book. I am deeply grateful for the intuitive spirit that illumines her vision and her wisdom.

I give thanks for my parents, Blanton and Margaret Whitmire, for their loving support, their willingness to read drafts, and for the example of their lives. I am especially thankful to the universe for my son, Zachary Hunter, whose presence illumines my life, and who began this project when he asked me to "write down those things that you say."

My greatest gratitude for this book is for my husband, Tom Ewell, who believed in the vision of this book, held me in prayer, and was a gifted editor. His mark is on every page. He is my dearest friend.

*Catherine Susan Whitmire*
*May 31, 2000*

When I discovered the Quaker tradition twenty-five years ago, "plain living" was the quality I found most compelling. So it is a great gift to me, and will prove a great gift to many others, that Cathy Whitmire has lifted up this central feature of Quakerism—and of human wholeness—in her lovely and lively book.

I can still feel the impact of my first Quaker meeting for worship, of the simplicity and quietude I experienced there. I was at a tumultuous point in my own life when I began attending those meetings: thirty-five years old, deeply conflicted about my calling, fearful of failing at familial and professional obligations—and covering it all with a bravado that made things even worse!

But when I walked into the meeting for worship on oak floorboards that glowed with the patina of age; when I sat on one of the simple wooden benches arranged in a squared circle at the heart of a century-old stone barn; when I settled into the silence with thirty or forty people, a silence that flowed on for an hour or so, rippled only occasionally by soulful speech; and when, as never before, I felt God's presence in the sunlight that came through the window and fell on the floor at my feet—then, what passed through me time and again was the peace that passes all understanding.

I do not want to suggest that plain living is all sweetness and light. The history of Quaker social action—from peacemaking to war relief to civil rights—reveals how simplicity can impel people to plunge into the world's most intractable problems. That is the point of the old story about a hapless stranger who accidentally entered a Quaker meeting for worship and waited patiently for someone to get things started. Five minutes he sat in silence, and then ten, and finally he could bear it no longer. Leaning toward the person next to him, the stranger whispered, "When does the service begin?" Answered the Quaker, "As soon as the worship ends."

Of course, what one ultimately confronts in simplicity and quietude is not only the world but one's self, especially the complexity and noise that many of us carry within. Plain living is unpopular in our society because frenzied living allows us to ignore, at least for a while, all our contradictions, duplicities, and self-deceptions. But when we quiet down, and guard our spirits against the distractions of conventional culture, we often discover that we have a lot to deal with—from finding right livelihood, to truing our relationships, to reaching out across great cultural divides.

No, plain living is not all sweetness and light, but neither is it all *sturm und drang*. I had a memorable Quaker friend named Ed Morgenroth who, during his eighty-plus years of life, was a vital force in early childhood education, prison reform, and interfaith relationships. In his elder years Morgen would exclaim, not infrequently, "I like simple living, and a lot of it!" In his exclamation are qualities of freedom, playfulness, and *joie de vivre* that we cannot possibly get from the costly commercial "entertainments" with which we are surrounded, qualities that come only from appreciating the elemental gift of life.

How easily we get trapped in that which is not essential—in looking good, winning at competition, gathering power and wealth—when simply being alive is the gift beyond measure. As I die, I rather doubt that I will be reviewing my prizes or my popularity or my bank account. I hope I will be gazing inwardly at that glorious patch of sun gleaming on an old oak floor, a window of light opening into the deep reality of life eternal. Living—just plain living—is the finest thing of all, and this good, good book will help all who read it stay centered on that truth.

*Parker J. Palmer*

(Parker J. Palmer's latest books are *Let Your Life Speak: Listening for the Voice of Vocation* and *The Courage to Teach: Exploring the Inner Landscape of a Teacher's Life.*)

# Introduction:
## Beginning a Path to Plain Living

Most of us living in this complex and time-pressured era have moments when we wish we were living simpler, more meaningful lives. Sometimes these wishes are just fleeting desires, but for many today the search for a life of greater simplicity and meaning has developed into a deep longing.

There are many routes to simplicity, but this book focuses on the spiritual path followed by members of the Religious Society of Friends, or Quakers. For 350 years Quakers have been living out of a spiritual center in a way of life they call "plain living." Their accumulated experience and distilled wisdom have much to offer those of us seeking greater simplicity today. This book tries to make their now well-worn path to plain living accessible to everyone.

My personal journey along the path of plain living began twenty-five years ago when I was an overextended health care administrator looking desperately for ways to simplify my life. I attended time management seminars, reorganized my office for greater efficiency, and even tried sleeping less. When there were still not enough hours in my long days to balance my commitments to family, work, and personal life, I developed an annual New Year's ritual of writing personal "management by objectives." I diligently wrote my relationship, financial, health, and spiritual goals for the new year, and then mapped out extensive strategies complete with time lines for how I planned to achieve them. I reasoned that if this planning process worked for me at the clinic, I should be able to apply it to my personal life. Throughout the year I would be comforted by looking at the detailed goals and elegant time lines in my journal. They gave me hope that by the end of the year my life would become simpler and more meaningful.

But my personal "management by objectives" strategy never seemed to work out, and I was increasingly perplexed. Why was I so busy and stressed? Why couldn't I simplify my life by careful planning? At the same time, I felt nudged by vague spiritual longings I couldn't identify which led me to question my personal goals. *What was I really seeking for my life?*

I persevered with my annual New Year's charts until a friend commented on my efforts by gently inquiring, "How do you know what God is planning for your life?" This was an intriguing question—and one that had not even occurred to me. As I look back now on those early efforts to plan and control my life, I am reminded of the advice of Quaker author Parker J. Palmer: "Before you tell your life what you intend to do with it, listen for what it intends to do with you."[1] Contemporary culture had taught me to look outward for answers, and so I had not thought to simplify my life by looking inward to my Center and listening to the longings of my heart.

As I learned to listen within and to focus my time and energies on what I discerned to be God's will instead of my own, my life began to simplify itself. I found I could let go of extraneous plans and possessions because they no longer fit what I now discerned to be the primary goals for my life at that time—a career change, a move, and more family time. Changes that had seemed difficult and complicated were suddenly clear. I had a series of garage sales, cut back on my hours at work, selected clothing and a hairstyle that were easier to maintain, chose a simpler and more natural plan for my front yard, etc. As a result, I found time to meditate every day, spent more time with my son, deepened friendships, and participated in community activities. *This simplification process was not about "sacrifice" but about choosing the life I really wanted.* I felt "lighter," and began to experience the joy and contentment I had longed for. I had made a first step toward Quaker "plain living."

As I continued to listen within and discern, I felt led to a career change that involved moving across the country. I knew I needed the advice and counsel of trusted friends who understood the spiritual basis of the changes I was making, so I called close friends and asked them to help me discern what my next steps should be. We gathered and they listened prayerfully. Their general counsel was that in their experience the more faithful we are to what we hear by listening within, the more likely we are to receive the wisdom and guidance our heart seeks. With their support, I found the courage to follow my leading. I moved across the country, began a graduate degree program, and chose a quieter pace of life that allowed me to have more time both for myself and for my family.

Over time I have cultivated the spiritual disciplines of attentiveness and contemplative listening. Of course my life has continued to have struggles and challenges, but my faith in what I hear when I listen within has deepened, and my trust in the process of shared discernment continues to grow. I still find it difficult to take a first step along a path when the step beyond is not clear, but I have found that when I trust this process of listening within there is always enough light for the next step.

*Through my personal journey I have come to understand plain living as a matter of spiritual intent, or an aim of the heart.* It consists of aligning our lives with what we hear when we listen to our Guide. It is learning to live our lives in "constant communication with that Center which is the source of life itself."[2] It is both a gift and a discipline. Early Quakers called this "staying close to the root."[3]

Plain living is a form of inward simplicity that leads us to listen for the "still, small voice" of God's claim upon our lives. It is both a spiritual lens and a discipline of holy obedience. This way of living simplifies our lives because when we focus our energies on what we discern by listening within, we are able to release the extraneous activities and possessions that clutter our path.

Living simply means adopting a lifestyle that avoids the unnecessary accumulation of material items, or what Quakers have often referred to as "cumber." It helps us seek outward detachment from the things of this world in order to focus our lives on the leadings of Spirit. Living simply entails clearing our lives and our houses of spiritual and material clutter so as to create more space for faithful living.

Since the 1650s, Quakers have been experimenting with a variety of spiritual practices to help them keep to the path of plain living. Their accounts of these experiments are recorded in the readings which are the basis of this book. Quakers have a long tradition of individually and corporately reading accounts of one another's spiritual journeys, reflecting on them, learning from them. This book tries to capture that rich tradition.

Another historic Quaker practice is the use of evocative reflection questions, or *queries*, similar to those found at the end of each section of this book. As used in this text, the queries are intended to engage the reader in reflection on the spiritual and ethical themes just presented.

This book is not about "six easy steps to plain living." There is no formula that works for everyone. I discovered long ago that life is both more abundant and more complex than that. Plain living is a spiritual journey of discovery, a path to be followed, not a goal to be achieved. It is not always an easy path to walk, but it does lead to deep contentment and a joy-filled way of living as witnessed by the serenity and grace which often characterizes the lives of elderly Quakers and others who have practiced plain living over many years. The quotations and stories in this book are all by and about Quakers, but the process of plain living they describe is universal and available to everyone.

### Editorial Notes on the Book

Quakerism was born in England in the 1650s, a time when English society was stratified by social class. The Quakers, however, believed that the Light of God shone equally in all people, so they refused to bow, use honorific titles, or doff their hats. They also offended the gentry by persistently using the grammatically familiar "thee" and "thou" in their addresses to all classes of people because it was consistent with their religious belief in equality. As a contemporary extension of this historic Quaker commitment to equality and "plain speech," the pronouns in this book have been adapted and are gender-inclusive.

I must make two brief disclaimers. First, there are several different branches of Quakerism. Although I have included quotations from a wide spectrum of Quaker authors, my selection of these quotations was influenced by my experience as a member of an unprogrammed (silent) meeting in New England.

Second, when reading selected writings from any group, it is easy to make that group appear wiser or more virtuous than their actual practice. So it is with these writings and the Quakers they represent. As Quaker elder John Wilhelm Rowntree once reminded Quakers, "We know better than we do."[4]

### Walking the Path

This book offers an invitation to discern for yourself the adventures and deep joy of a life of plain living. Everything needed to embark on this path is already within you. It is the journey of a lifetime, and for those who are just beginning, Quaker mystic Thomas Kelly advises:

Open your eyes to the flaming vision
of the wonder of such a life.
Begin where you are. Now.
If you slip and stumble,
don't spend too much time in anguished regrets
and self-accusations but begin again.
Don't grit your teeth and clench your fists and say,
"I will! I will!" Relax.
Take hands off. Submit yourself to God. . . .
Let life be willed through you.[5]

Blessings on your journey!

# CHAPTER 1

# Keeping to Plainness

## by Choosing

## Inward Simplicity

## Simple Living

It has never been easy to lay down an encumbered lifestyle. In the 1600s William Penn, the founder of Pennsylvania, struggled with "cumber" during his conversion from English aristocrat to plain Quaker. He began attending Quaker meetings in courtly apparel, wearing a powdered wig and carrying a sword. The more time William spent with the plainly dressed Quakers, however, the more uncomfortable he became with the clothes he was wearing and the way he was living.

Legend has it that when William asked pacifist George Fox, the founder of the Quakers, what to do about carrying his sword, Fox replied, "Wear it as long as thee can." Fox believed that William would know when it was time to choose a plainer and more peaceful way of living.[6] Later on, according to an old journal, William was horseback riding with a Friend when he "suddenly pulled off his (courtly) wig, dropped it on the road, and did not look back to see what became of it."[7]

When we listen within, we too may hear an invitation to lay down our encumbered lifestyle. It is as difficult a decision now as it was in the 1600s. Contemporary life surrounds us with a whirlwind of constant noise, incessant activity, and meaningless clutter, so it is not surprising that most of us are overextended, chronically tired, and feel weighed down by the pressures we carry. We have chosen lives that crowd our appointment books, fill our e-mail boxes, and overload our answering machines, even as we long for a plainer way of living—one that will free us from the strain and anxiety of these times. The Spirit is speaking through the whirlwind of modern life, and if we listen quietly to the cool, calm Center within, there is an invitation to plain living awaiting each of us.

The simple life is one in which there is always time to remember the divine purpose behind each of our tasks, time to listen for a possible divine amendment to the day's schedule, and time to be thankful for the divine presence at each moment of the day.

*Lloyd Lee Wilson, 1993*

. . . Simplification comes when we "center down,"
when life is lived with singleness of eye,
from a holy Center
where the breath and stillness of Eternity
are heavy upon us and
we are wholly yielded to God.
Some of you know this holy,
recreating Center of eternal peace and joy
and live in it day and night.
Some of you may see it over the margin and
wistfully long
to slip into that amazing Center
where the soul is at home with God.
Be very faithful to that wistful longing.
It is the Eternal Goodness calling you to return Home.

*Thomas R. Kelly, 1941*

It may surprise some of us to hear that the first generation of Friends did not have a testimony for simplicity. They came upon a faith which cut to the root of the way they saw life, radically reorienting it. They saw that all they did must flow directly from what they experienced as true, and that if it did not, both the knowing and the doing became false. In order to keep the knowledge clear and the doing true, they stripped away anything which seemed to get in the way. They called those things superfluities, and it is this radical process of stripping for clear-seeing which we now term simplicity.

*Frances Irene Taber, 1985*

Simplification of our lives
results from centering down,
from living our lives
in constant communication
with that Center which is
the source of life itself.

*T. Canby Jones, 1988*

The last fruit of holy obedience is the simplicity of the trusting child, the simplicity of the children of God. It is the simplicity which lies beyond complexity. It is the naivete which is the yonder side of sophistication. It is the beginning of spiritual maturity, which comes after the awkward age of religious busyness for the Community of God—yet how many are caught and arrested in development, within this adolescent development of the soul's growth! The mark of this simplified life is radiant joy. . . . Knowing sorrow to the depths it does not agonize and fret and strain, but in serene, unhurried calm it walks in time with the joy and assurance of Eternity.

*Thomas R. Kelly, 1941*

Each must determine in the light that is given what promotes and what hinders our compelling search for the Commonwealth of God. The call to each is to abandon those things that clutter life and to press toward the goal unhampered. This is true simplicity.

*Ohio Valley Yearly Meeting, 1977*

QUERIES

- *Do I make time in my life to remember the divine purpose behind each of my tasks?*

- *Do I seek to simplify my life by listening for guidance from an inward holy center?*

- *What promotes and what hinders my search for inward simplicity?*

Keep in all modesty and plainness . . .
For they that follow those things,
that the world's spirit invents daily
cannot be solid.

*George Fox, 1667*

Quakers have long since discarded the Quaker gray, the broad-brimmed hat, the Quaker bonnet, which were once their distinguishing marks. Other Quaker ways have disappeared, too. If modern Friends use "thee" it is only within their immediate family. The prohibition against art, music, and theater is regarded as the sad mistake of another age. Quakers, a predominantly middle-class group, share the tastes and interests of most middle-class Americans.

And yet one Quaker can usually recognize another in a crowd. There is a penchant for a simple, direct style of dress, a habit of understatement, and a directness of approach which most Quakers share. . . . The years of isolation, of persecution, and of the championing of lost causes have developed among Quakers a family feeling rather unusual in the modern world.

*Margaret Hope Bacon, 1969*

Outwardly, simplicity is shunning superfluities of dress, speech, behavior, and possessions, which tend to obscure our vision of reality. Inwardly, simplicity is spiritual detachment from the things of this world as part of the effort to fulfill the first commandment: to love God with all of the heart and mind and strength.

The testimony of outward simplicity began as a protest against the extravagance and snobbery which marked English society in the 1600s. In whatever forms this protest is maintained today, it must still be seen as a testimony against involvement with things which tend to dilute our energies and scatter our thoughts, reducing us to lives of triviality and mediocrity.

Simplicity does not mean drabness or narrowness but is essentially positive, being the capacity for selectivity in one who holds attention on the goal. Thus simplicity is an appreciation of all that is helpful towards living as children of the living God.

*North Carolina Yearly Meeting*
*(Conservative), 1983*


Simplicity is not so much about what we own, but about what owns us. If we need lots of possessions to maintain our self-esteem and create our self-image and to look good to our neighbors, then we have forgotten or neglected that which is real and inward. If our time, money, and energy are consumed in selecting, acquiring, maintaining, cleaning, moving, improving, replacing, dusting, storing, using, showing off, and talking about our possessions, then there is little time, money, and energy left for our other pursuits such as the work we do to further the Community of God.

*Christin Hadley Snyder, 1991*


We must sit light to our possessions lest they come to possess us. Used as sales-talk in our glossy magazines, the phrase "gracious living" has become a synonym for making a house an end in itself rather than a home to live in. Truly gracious living is a by-product of gracious thinking and doing, and in material things is expressed in "what is simple and beautiful." And true simplicity is not the rejection of beauty in our surroundings, but the refusal to allow concern for things to clutter our minds. . . .

*Edgar B. Castle, 1961*


Creative simplicity involves developing our own tastes, rather than letting them be formed by advertising and other social pressures which stunt imagination and discourage self-expression. Simple living is a rediscovery of our creative and imaginative energies.

*The Simple Living Collective, 1974*

Simplicity does not mean
getting rid of all of your possessions,
but rather integrating them
into your life's purpose.

*From a talk by Mary Gregory as
remembered by Emily Sander, 2000*

Simplicity, when it removes encumbering details, makes for beauty in music, in art, and in living. It clears the springs of life and permits wholesome mirth and gladness to bubble up; it cleans the windows of life and lets joy radiate. It requires the avoidance of artificial or harmful social customs and conventions, but it opens wide the door to cultivate and express to all sincere cordiality, kindness, and friendliness. This sort of simplicity removes barriers and eases tensions. In its presence all can be at ease.

*Philadelphia Yearly Meeting, 1961*

If simplicity of living is a valid principle, there is one important precaution and condition of its application. I can explain it best by something which Mahatma Gandhi said to me. We were talking about simple living, and I said that it was easy for me to give up most things but that I had a greedy mind and wanted to keep my many books. He said, "Then don't give them up. As long as you derive inner help and comfort from anything, you should keep it. If you were to give it up in a mood of self-sacrifice or out of a stern sense of duty, you would continue to want it back, and that unsatisfied want would make trouble for you. Only give up a thing when you want some other condition so much that the thing no longer has any attraction for you, or when it seems to interfere with that which is more greatly desired."

*Richard Gregg, 1936*

In real life, it is hard to avoid complexity and contradiction—even Thoreau, while living at Walden Pond, had his mother do his laundry—but there is no one formula, no laundry list, that pinpoints the meaning of simple living. Nor is there an absolute standard by which simplicity can be measured; what is simple for one person may for others be either Byzantine or hopelessly idealistic. The choices each person makes are conditioned by how he or she defines simplicity and by circumstances that are invariably singular.

*Frank Levering and Wanda Urbanska, 1992*

Still another step toward simplicity is to refuse to live beyond our means emotionally. In a culture where whirl is king, we must understand our emotional limits. Ulcers, migraines, nervous tension, and a dozen other symptoms mark our psychic overload. We are concerned not to live beyond our means financially; why do it emotionally?

*Richard J. Foster, 1981*

. . . I seek simplicity of mind by trusting myself. I waste so much energy in doubting. I must quit this unending Self-Doubt (in Native [American] circles called "Sincrime"), not so much because I'm strong and spiritually together, but because it's simpler. I don't have time or energy to go on roller coaster rides of despair and self-doubt. . . . I seek simplicity of mind by trusting others to take care of themselves. I waste too much energy in co-dependency, worrying about others' troubles—the "save the world" syndrome. It can clear the mind by not taking on the distractions, worries, fears, and moods of others. Letting things pass through. Not taking on things that are not ours to carry.

*Dorothy Mack, 1997*

All joy arises from a sense of *being*,
while the main emphasis in our society is on *having*. . . .

*Damaris Parker-Rhodes, 1985*

There is no fixed standard of simplicity.
What is very simple for one person often seems
very complex and extravagant for another person.
There is no known calculus of simplicity.

*Rufus M. Jones, 1940*

QUERIES

- *In what ways do I allow my possessions to determine my sense of worth and self-esteem?*

- *Am I careful not to live beyond my financial or emotional means?*

- *What criteria do I use to determine what constitutes simplicity for me?*

# CHAPTER 2

# Beginning With Ourselves and Our

Work

Time

Integrity

Plain Speech

Money and Resources

In 1763, John Woolman felt led by a "motion of love" to visit Native Americans living along the banks of the Susquehanna River in Pennsylvania. During his visit in a remote village, Woolman was invited to worship with his native hosts. When he stood to pray, he silently motioned the interpreter who rose with him to stay seated so that his words would go untranslated. After the service, Papunehaug, one of the tribe's leaders, said to Woolman's interpreter, "I love to feel where the words come from."[8]

There is a deep well within each of us that can only be filled by the Holy, and the motions of love that emanate from those depths are the roots of our integrity. Whether spoken or felt, these ripples are the source of our deepest truth and the way God communicates with us deep to deep. Because Woolman's prayer came from this hallowed place, Papunehaug could trust the integrity of the words even when he could not understand their meaning.

We are not called to conform to the ways of the world, but to the motions of love that rise in our hearts. It takes courage to align our personal lives, our work, and the way we spend our days with what we hear when we listen within. We live in cynical times, and we have become skeptical people: openly lied to by those we elect, betrayed by those who put greed before compassion, and robbed of a healthy Earth by a lifestyle that is not sustainable. We often no longer know who to listen to or what to believe.

The integrity we are seeking lies within the sanctum of our individual and corporate souls. It is there we must struggle with moral complexity and the consequences of the values we adopt. Plain living is about trusting "the place the words come from" and aligning our lives and our integrity accordingly.

The Bible story begins with emphasis on God as worker, in making the world, and then stresses the creation of humans in God's image. If God is the Worker, then men and women, in order to fulfill their potentialities, must be workers, too. They are sharing in creation when they develop a farm, paint a picture, build a home, or polish a floor.

*Elton Trueblood, 1993*

In every situation seek to be aware of the presence of God, praying that spiritual energies in yourself and in others may be released for the furtherance of God's community. Life brings many conflicting responsibilities and choices. To some, the summons may come to apply fresh energy and vision to their present work; to others to make a complete change, perhaps even to retire early or limit their engagements, so that they may be free for new service of God's appointing. When you have a choice of employment, choose that which gives the fullest opportunity for the use of your talents in the service of God and humanity.

*Canadian Yearly Meeting, 1969*

What seems important to me is not what a person does, but how they do it. Do salespeople artificially stimulate a need, or do they put themselves in the position of their customer to help them understand and obtain what they really want? Do lawyers batten on the paranoid fears of their clients, or are they a constant witness to the peace testimony as they mediate between ferocious litigants? Do doctors believe in sickness or in health? Are teachers dedicated time-servers, or do they love their subject and respond with pleasure to the growth of their students? Do administrators manipulate people to get them to do what they want, or are they a clerk of the meeting releasing the vitality of their equals in a way useful to the group? Do homemakers go through a repetitious succession of menial tasks, or do they build a loving community? Such questions can be asked of every occupation.

*George Peck, 1973*

At root, a professional is one who makes a profession of faith—
faith in something larger and wiser than his or her powers.

*Parker J. Palmer, 1990*

To pray about any day's work
does not mean to ask for success in it. . . .
It means to see "my" work as part of a whole,
to see myself as not mattering much, but my faith,
the energy, will and striving, which I put into the work,
as mattering a great deal. My faith is the point in me
at which God comes into my work;
through faith the work is given dignity and value.

*Mary F. Smith, 1936*

The nurture of spirituality within organizations begins with spiritually grounded and spiritually liberated leadership. Leaders
whose vision arises from their discernment of God's will, and
who are motivated by their commitment to be faithful to that
understanding, are focused on something beyond themselves.
They are attuned to, and trusting of, something beyond the organization; beyond, yet encompassing the hearts and souls that are
counted within its sphere. Their principles are grounded in religious values and the organizational processes they create, offer,
and nurture within the organization are rooted in those values.
Such grounded leaders are liberated by a willingness to rely on
their spiritual instincts, trusting that their gifts are serving to realize a vision. The fruits of their faithfulness can be evidenced in
the development and support of a community that embraces its
mission, is open to change, and that fosters mutuality among its
members. Such an organization, though never achieving perfec-
tion, offers a quality of service that its constituents experience as
wholesome, caring, and respectful of individual concerns.

*Margaret Benefiel and Rebecca Darden
Phipps, 1999*

Let your lives speak.

*George Fox, 1652*

We can best discover the principle of the simple life by a contrast with the spirit of commercialism. The commercial spirit is selfish. Its motto is "Expand to get." . . . Over and against it, at its antipodes, is the spirit of the simple life. It can be lived at any level of poverty or wealth; and at any stage of ignorance or culture. It is essentially the spirit of living for life's sake, or consecration to personal and social goodness. This spirit does not keep us out of commercial business, nor does it command us to confine our business to narrow limits and to small returns. But if we are to belong to the goodly fellowship of those who live the simple life, our business must be made an avenue of ministering to human life.

*Rufus M. Jones, 1927*

QUERIES

- Does my work and sense of vocation come from a process of inner discernment?

- Do I pray about my work?

- Do I make my work, whatever it may be, an avenue for doing good?

Ye have no time but this present time,
therefore prize your time for your soul's sake.

George Fox, 1652

We breathe the air of a generation which,
as the old phrase goes,
"takes time seriously."
People nowadays take time
far more seriously than eternity.

Thomas R. Kelly, 1938

Time is one of God's gifts which we easily take for granted, and in the use of which we are commonly prodigal. It is rich in opportunities, yet it is relentless in its record of our selection. According to the way we spend the minutes and hours we will find the Divine Spirit within us coming into possession or being crowded out of our lives.

Philadelphia Yearly Meeting, 1927

Boredom with the ongoing grind of the real world leads to predictable responses: "Let's rent a video/go shopping/surf the Internet." Spiritual seeking leads to a bunch of uncomfortable questions: "Why am I bored? What void is this boredom telling me I need to fill? What will I discover if I just try to sit through my boredom?" Most days, most of us would rather rent a video than wrestle with our soul's hunger for meaning. . . .

Henry Sessions, 1999

So I don't spend much time with the radio, television, and the daily paper. A car without a radio is a place for contemplation. When friends object that I don't know what is going on and am not concerned with the life of our society, I answer that they are deluded. History does not happen by the day. Once I read every copy of a leading newspaper from January to September 1870, with the intention of discovering the nature of the historical forces of that period. What I did discover was a host of superficialities, fleeting illusions, and enormous blind spots as to what was really going on. . . .

*George Peck, 1973*

Many of you are in easy circumstances, and some of you are exposed to the dangers and temptations of affluence. May you now, in the bloom of your days, think of the importance of a well-spent life! . . . Consider how you are spending your time. Is it to advance the cause of truth and righteousness, or is it merely to gratify yourselves?

*Henry Hull, 1812*

Within all of us is a whole conglomerate of selves. There is the timid self, the courageous self, the business self, the parental self, the religious self, the literary self, the energetic self. All of these selves are rugged individualists. No bargaining or compromise for them. Each one screams to protect his or her vested interests. If a decision is made to spend a relaxed evening listening to Chopin, the business self and the civic self rise up in protest at the loss of precious time. . . .

No wonder we feel distracted and torn. . . . But when we experience life at the Center, all is changed. Our many selves come under the unifying control of the divine Arbitrator. No longer are we forced to live by an inner majority rule which always leaves a disgruntled minority. The divine Yes or No settles all minority reports.

*Richard J. Foster, 1981*

As we learn to see ourselves as part of Gaia, the great living entity that is our planet, we begin to see how we have wasted our lives in frantic, exhausting efforts to get ahead and to protect our status and power over others. How spiritually corrupting to play the game of one-upmanship! As life becomes more relaxed, we find we are healed in body and in spirit.

'Tis a gift to be simple, 'tis a gift to be free,
'Tis a gift to come down where we ought to be. . . .

*Elizabeth Watson, 1991*

Much of our acceptance of multitudes of obligations is due to our inability to say No. We calculated that that task had to be done, and we saw no one ready to undertake it. . . . But when we say Yes or No to calls, on the basis of inner guidance and whispered promptings of encouragement from the Center of our life, or on the basis of a lack of any inward "rising" of that Life to encourage us in the call, we have no reason to give, except one—the will of God as we discern it.

*Thomas R. Kelly, 1939*

In religious circles we find today a fierce and almost violent planning and programming. A sense that without ceaseless activity nothing will ever be accomplished. How seldom it occurs to us that God has to undo and to do all over again so much of what we in our willfulness have pushed through in God's name. How little there is in us of the silent and radiant strength in which the secret works of God really take place! How ready we are to speak, how loath to listen, to sense the further dimension of what it is that we confront.

*Douglas Steere, 1962*

Time, as sheer flow, is tantalizing, torturing, tragedy. Time as experienced in its matrix and seedbed, the Eternal, is perpetual completion, triumph, release. Time as ever-stretched toward goals is endless disappointment and postponements; Time as continuously given within and flowing from the Eternal is charged with serenity and satisfaction. Were earthly life to end in this moment, all would be well.

For this Here, this Now, is not a mathematical point in the stream of Time; it is swollen with Eternity, it is the dwelling place

of God. We ask no more; we are at home. Thou who hast made
us for Thyself dost in each moment give us our rest in Thee.

*Thomas R. Kelly, 1938*

To think of one's life as
time to be invested or
to sacrifice the present
to an uncertain future
is foolishness . . .
it is obvious that life is a gift
rather than a reward. . . .

*Jim Corbett, 1991*

How do I dwell in the eternity of the moment?
By letting the eternity of the moment dwell in me.

*Damaris Parker-Rhodes, 1977*

There is also a vision of divine order which does not require each
of us to take on everything. There is a sense that in a world under
gospel order, or divine guidance, each person's appointed tasks
would fit together organically, moving toward God's unknowable
goals for the universe. There is a sense that we are not responsible for the outcome. We are responsible for faithfully discerning
and performing our own personal parts in the process, leaving the
outcome to God.

*Patricia Loring, 1992*

QUERIES

❧ Do I prize my time as a gift from God?

❧ When I feel frustrated with "not having enough time," do I ask my Inner
Guide for direction?

❧ Do I arrange time in my daily schedule for quiet time and reflection that
can help me grow into the person my Inner Guide hopes I will
become?

Integrity for me means my outward actions line up
like a plumb line to God who is present
in my deepest Center.

*Janet Hoffman, 1992*

The root meaning of the word "integrity" calls for wholeness. The word comes from the Latin *integritas*, which refers to a state or quality of being complete, that is a condition of wholeness. The word "integrity" and the mathematical term "integer" have a common meaning. When we look at this common meaning of *integritas*, or "integrity," it points to a unity, that, when applied to persons, we call community. Integrity creates a sense of togetherness and belonging when applied to persons in community. Integrity forms the basis for a covenant relationship in which persons exercise a sense of responsibility and accountability toward one another.

We need to begin to live the way we want the world to become, rather than the way the world is now. . . .

*Wilmer A. Cooper, 1991*

[The Kenyan Joel] Litu served first in a court tribunal in Mbale, his home village, among his own people. It did not take long before his integrity was tested. One day a man seeking a favor followed Litu to his house in Mbale. The man came late in the evening when it was getting dark. Under his right arm he carried a large hen. . . . Joel spoke first:

"Eh! What is new! Where are you from?" "I am from my home" the man replied. "What do you have to say then?" asked Joel. "I thought I should come to see you about the case," said the man moving closer. "Eh! Where did you get that huge hen?" asked Joel. "Oh! My Lord, I thought I would give it to you," the man answered enthusiastically, moving even closer. As if stung by a bee, Litu used a sharp voice: "Ah! Ah! Stand where you are. . . . Take the hen away, then come very early in the morning and tell me the whole story at the court. As for the hen, go with it in peace!" The man stood there for some time, hesitating, then asked, "I wonder, did you say I should go?" "Go away," Litu said, "Oh! Marita, why don't you open that hen house for this man to see all the hens we have!"

Such was his plain refusal of bribes. Word soon spread about the Quaker man who would not accept bribes in court cases.

*Rose Adede, 1982*


Refusing to face moral complexity
can be a form of running away,
or refusing to face
the necessarily unpleasant
consequences of the values we adopt.
It can amount to an attempt to avoid
our personal Gethsemane.

*John Punshon, 1990*


A neighbor received a bad bruise on his body, and sent for me to bleed him; which being done, he desired me to write his will. I took notes, and among other things, he told me to which of his children he gave his young Negro. I considered the pain and distress he was in, and knew not how it would end, so I wrote his will, save only that part concerning his slave, and carrying it to his bedside, read it to him, and then told him, in a friendly way, that I could not write any instruments by which my fellow-creatures were made slaves, without bringing trouble on my own mind. I let him know that I charged nothing for what I had done, and desired to be excused from doing the other part in the way he proposed. Then we had a serious conference on the subject, and at length, he agreeing to set her free, I finished his will.

*John Woolman, 1756*


. . . Real values are not learned.
They form.
They form from inside out.
They cannot be imposed.

*Alfred K. LaMotte, 1982*

When the draft came, Bayard Rustin (1912–1987) was granted conscientious objector status because he was a Quaker and was assigned hospital work. But, when a similarly scrupulous Methodist was turned down [for conscientious objector status], Bayard's integrity would not allow him to accept his option of alternative service work in the hospital. Instead, for reasons of integrity, Bayard chose to spend the next twenty-eight months in federal penitentiaries.

*Based on information from Hugh Barbour, et al., 1995*

The Truth is one and the same always,
and though ages and generations pass away,
and one generation goes and another comes,
yet the word and power and spirit of the Living God
endures forever, and is the same and never changes.

*Margaret Fell, 1660*

. . . [Quakers] live out a corporate integrity that is not the sum of the individual truths of its constituent parts, but a truth revealed to the corporate body gathered in worship.

*Janet Hoffman, 1991*

At the end of an hour of worship in August 1968, the Clerk of the Friends Meeting at Cambridge, Massachusetts, rose and introduced Eric Rutan, who was absent-without-leave (AWOL) from the army because he could not, in conscience, go to Vietnam. She said, "We who oppose all war are associating ourselves with certain young men who have refused to comply with the draft or to fight in Vietnam."

The Meeting called a press conference to announce that until Eric (who was not a Quaker) was arrested, a group of Quakers would worship with him twenty-four hours a day in the Meetinghouse. Friends made food, set up beds, and continued to worship around the clock for two and a half weeks. When federal officers arrived with a warrant, Eric was sitting in worship at the front of the room, near the fireplace. No one in the hushed room gave any sign that the police officers were different from all the others who'd come to worship for the past weeks. The officers seemed to sense the depth of the worship and sat down quietly on a bench towards the back of the room.

The worship continued, unbroken by their entrance. . . . A Friend rose and spoke quietly of Friends' willingness to suffer rather than to kill anyone, since to kill a person was to kill part of God. After more worship, Eric left with the officers. The prayer continued for another quarter of an hour, then Friends shook hands to end their long period of worship.

*Based on information from Daisy Newman,*
*1972*

When a young Florence Kelly (1859–1932), later the head of the National Consumers League, observed that her aunt, Sarah Pugh, never used sugar or products made of cotton, Florence asked her aunt about this and later recorded her impressions of the conversation:

"Cotton was grown by slaves, and sugar also," my aunt replied, "so I decided many years ago never to use either, and to bring these facts to the attention of my friends."

Not meaning to be impertinent, I said, "Aunt Sarah, does thee really think any slaves were freed because thee did not use sugar or cotton?"

Perfectly tranquil was her reply: "Dear child, I can never know that any slave was personally helped, but I had to live with my own conscience."

*Based on information from Carol and John*
*Stoneburner, 1986*

QUERIES

🖎 *How do I recognize and deal with moral complexity in my daily life?*

🖎 *How do I contribute to the corporate integrity of the communities of which I am a part?*

🖎 *Am I living by values that will help create a better, more sustainable future for the world?*

Plainness also involves speech, not just special words, but `speaking so as to mean what we say. That means avoiding both sarcasm—saying the opposite of what one means—and also excessive politeness, or "beating around the bush."

*Susan Smith, 1984*

. . . Develop a habit of plain honest speech.
Strike "I am starved" from your speaking vocabulary.
When you are hungry say that you are hungry and
reserve the word "starvation" for the real thing.
Make honesty and integrity
the distinguishing characteristics of your speech.
Reject jargon and abstract speculation,
the purpose of which is to obscure and impress
rather than to illuminate and inform.

*Richard J. Foster, 1981*

Dispatch business quickly,
and keep out of long debates and heats . . .
be swift to hear,
and slow to speak,
and let it be in the grace,
which seasons all words.

*George Fox, 1690*

In a public meeting I once spoke of a fellow pastor as "the most capable and compassionate pastor I know." Later this good friend confronted me about the statement, saying that he did not feel compassion was yet a distinguishing characteristic of his ministry. He was helping me to see the difference between a true compliment and sheer flattery. A compliment affirms what is already there or coming into being. Flattery degrades us by saying something is that isn't.

*Richard J. Foster, 1981*

William Bown (1735–1824) was born a slave, was later freed, and is remembered for his plain and truthful speaking. A wealthy white neighbor of Bown's frequently availed himself of William's obliging disposition by borrowing his grindstone instead of procuring one for himself. One day when this neighbor asked William for the use of his grindstone, William returned the usual compliment of saying he was welcome, but after the man was gone, William became uneasy in his mind with his reply, because he knew it to be insincere. He went to his neighbor's and acknowledged that, although he had told his neighbor that he was welcome, it was only in conformity with custom, and was not the truth. William said that he felt his neighbor could more easily afford to keep a grindstone of his own than he (William) could. . . .

*Based on information from Kenneth Ives, 1986*

The testimony of simplicity was a result of
the effort not only to speak but to live the truth.

*Elise Boulding, 1989*

Friends are credited with introducing the convention of the fixed price in retailing and the reduction of bargaining. Friends evidently felt that bargaining could not be done without lying, saying you were going to do something when actually you were prepared to do something else. Quaker shopkeepers and merchants, therefore, adopted the custom of the fixed price, leaving it up to the buyer as to whether to buy at that price.

*Kenneth E. Boulding, 1986*

QUERIES

- Are honesty and integrity distinguishing characteristics of my speech?

- Am I swift to hear and slow to speak, avoiding long, heated debates?

- Am I careful to say what I mean, avoiding sarcasm, excessive politeness, and self-aggrandizement designed to impress others?

The concept of stewardship as I use it here goes far beyond its common use as shorthand for charitable giving. It expresses both the notion that what is mine legally is not really mine, and its corollary that my custody of wealth imposes on me an obligation to use it responsibly. It is a rich concept that weighs on me more heavily each year, as I become more and more aware of how blessed I am with this world's goods.

*Kingdon W. Swayne, 1985*

When we are centrally placed in the richest nation in the history of the earth, moving beyond our anxieties about scarcity has both psychological and sociological dimensions. At root, however, it is a spiritual problem. To live in anxiety over scarcity when we have sufficient for our needs is to have missed somehow the overflowing generosity of God's abundance that has always been and always will be present for us—as well as our unity with one another.

This is not a promise that we will be at the top of the heap as God's economically chosen people. It is, however, an invitation to a sense of the freedom and richness of Life under, around, through, and among us when we are blessed with modest sufficiency. It is an invitation to participate in God's own overflowing abundance by sharing what we have with those who have less—whether materially or less tangibly: our time, our energy, our caring, our food, our possessions, our money. It's an invitation to love as freely and unconditionally as God has loved us. It's an invitation to generosity.

*Patricia Loring, 1997*

Like the words *ecumenical* and *ecology*, economics is rooted in the Greek word *oikos*, meaning *household*, and signifies the management of the household—arranging what is necessary for well-being. Good economic practice—positive ways of exchanging goods and services—is about the well-being, the livelihood, of the whole household. . . . While the notion of "home" in

American culture has shrunk from meaning one's town or region to meaning only one's own house or apartment, at the same time, paradoxically, it has become less possible to isolate our individual households from the world around them. As we try to defend the security of our private home, we are simultaneously rediscovering the economic-ecological truth of our profound interdependence within the small planet home we share.

*Sharon Daloz Parks, 1997*

In many ways those of European background in the United States still live with the mindset of Columbus. We believe that we are the greatest nation on earth; our democratic government and capitalist economic system represent the acme of civilization. Our political and economic interests are of the utmost importance and we are justified in exercising some control over the rest of the world, making war where our economic interest requires it, and covertly overthrowing governments not in our orbit. And like Columbus and his friends, we are driven by greed. The bottom line is more important than human need and the fate of the earth.

*Elizabeth Watson, 1992*

Money has many of the characteristics of deity. It gives us security, can induce guilt, gives us freedom, gives us power, and seems to be omnipresent. Most sinister of all, however, is its bid for omnipotence. It is money's desire for omnipotence, for all power, that seems so strange, so out of place. It seems that money is not willing to rest contented in its proper place alongside other things we value. No, it must have supremacy. It must crowd out all else. This is, I say, the strange thing about money. We attach importance to it far beyond its worth.

*Richard J. Foster, 1995*

John D. Rockefeller was once asked how much money it would take to be really satisfied. He answered, "Just a little bit more!" And that is precisely our problem—it always takes a little more;

contentment always remains elusive. But the wonderful thing about simplicity is its ability to give us contentment. . . . To live in contentment means we can opt out of the status race and the maddening pace that is its necessary partner. We can shout "No!" to the insanity which chants, "More, more, more!" We can rest contented in the gracious provision of God. . . .

*Richard J. Foster, 1981*

Much of our pain, sorrow, and wastefulness are the bitter consequences of our selfishness. The contemporary agonies of wars, poverty, social injustices, inflation, and environmental pollution are caused by greed. . . . Our love of possessions and the pursuit of financial security thwart our spiritual development. We slip into a subtle form of idolatry that robs us of fully becoming what we are created to be. . . .

*David Stanfield, undated document from the Quaker Collection at Haverford College, believed to have been written between 1962 and 1974*

We plunge ourselves into enormous debt and then take two and three jobs to stay afloat. We uproot our families with unnecessary moves just so we can have a more prestigious house. We grasp and grab and never have enough. And most destructive of all, our flashy cars and sports spectaculars and backyard pools have a way of crowding out much interest in civil rights or inner city poverty or the starved masses of India. Greed has a way of severing the cords of compassion.

*Richard J. Foster, 1981*

May we look upon our treasure, the furniture of our houses, and our garments, and try to discover whether the seeds of war have nourishment in these our possessions.

*John Woolman, 1774*

A wealthy woman informed me that she could never take a vacation for more than a few days because of the need to care for her investments, and that she simply had to have money since without it, she would have no friends. . . . Money, instead of being looked on as a useful tool, is widely regarded as a separate commodity and its ownership as an end in itself.

*S. Francis Nicholson, 1990*

## Emerging Economic Guidelines for the Common Good

~ "Communal property" (including the natural environment) is for the benefit of all.

~ Ostentation in material things is to be avoided.

~ Occupations and professions that deflect from the commitment to the community's life and witness are to be avoided.

~ The profit motive in economic transactions is to be held in relationship to other motivations and outcomes.

~ Mutual aid should be distinguished from charity, and resources shared in ways that recognize interdependence with others rather than fostering the perpetual dependence of many on a few.

*Sharon Daloz Parks, 1997, adapted from the Mennonite tradition*

Christian stewardship . . . is spontaneous, creative, free from the desire to obtain something in return. Such experiences of God's gracious (unmerited) love prompts us to re-order our scale of values from that of contemporary society to the one demonstrated by Jesus.

*David Stanfield, undated document from the Quaker Collection at Haverford College, believed to have been written between 1962 and 1974*

To me, the concepts of "stewardship" and "simplicity" have always seemed so closely related as to be almost identical: to practice one properly, it seems, one must always also practice the other. Nervertheless, there are differences. Simplicity deals with the ownership of property, stewardship with the use of it. Simplicity tells us to ask for no more than we need; stewardship reminds us that we need less if we take care of what we have. Simplicity insists that we get rid of encumbrances; stewardship helps us decide what are encumbrances and what are not. It does this in a very straightforward way. If a possession, or a task, is an encumbrance, using it properly readily becomes much more trouble than it is worth, and the possession falls into disrepair, or the task remains constantly undone. It is at this point that stewardship says, "Wait a minute—we have too much to take care of here," and it becomes time, in the good Quaker phrase, to lay something down.

*William Ashworth, 1986*

Those of us who are rich in this world's goods should not be proud: our riches are not a reward for anything that we have done. But neither should we be crippled by guilt. Paul tells us that our riches give us an opportunity to do good and to grow rich in noble actions; that we must be ready to give away and to share. So we must see our riches not as a reward for somehow being good, but as an opportunity for doing good. As Paul writes elsewhere (2 Corinthians 9:11), "You will always be rich enough to be generous."

*Tom and Liz Gates, 1995*

By the curious arithmetic of love,
the more we share, the more we possess;
the more we willingly give,
the more we multiply.

*Lowell E. Wright, undated document from the Quaker Collection at Haverford College*

QUERIES

☙ Do I prayerfully discern how to use my financial resources for the common good?

☙ Do I look at my investments, clothing, furniture, and other possessions to see if they sow the seeds of war and oppression?

☙ What criteria do I use to evaluate how much financial security is enough for me?

CHAPTER 3

# Plain Living Day by Day in

## Committed Relationships

## Parenting and Mentoring

## Aging

## Humor, Joy, and Gratitude

Over his desk in Bar Harbor, Maine, Ed Snyder, Executive Secretary Emeritus of Friends Committee on National Legislation, has a photograph of a jet plane trailing a white plume across a magnificently colored sky. Ed keeps the picture there to remind him of a particularly memorable message he once heard during meeting for worship. The Friend who delivered the message had worked in Saudi Arabia and told about a time his family had driven out into the desert to enjoy a picnic in the cool of the evening. A resplendent sunset of breathtaking beauty filled the wide horizon when across the brilliant colors "came a jet so distant that they could see nothing but the plume of the contrail against the sky." This Friend said he "thought about the passengers on the plane—eating, sleeping, reading, absorbed in their own private thoughts or conversations. Probably almost all were completely oblivious to what was happening just outside the cabin window." The speaker then reflected, "They were passing through Glory, and they didn't even know it."[9]

Glory surrounds us from birth. It encircles us as we draw air for our first tentative wail, and enfolds us after we empty our lungs for the last time. And in between these two breaths we dwell in the midst of this glory: in the joys and struggles of our personal relationships, the delights and challenges of nurturing children, the wisdom and suffering of aging, the detachment of death, the heartbreak of grief. And through it all we are sustained by keeping our eyes wide open to the wonder that is always around us.

The opportunity before us in every moment is to choose to live awakened lives—as children of awe, truly alive in the midst of the simple grandeur that surrounds our days. The art of plain living is to engage life as a process of opening our hearts and maintaining a vigilant awareness of the streams of glory encircling our lives.

We thank God, then, for the pleasures, joys, and triumphs of [life together]: for the cups of tea we bring each other, and the seedlings in the garden frame; for the domestic drama of meetings and partings, sickness and recovery; for the grace of occasional extravagance, flowers on birthdays and unexpected presents; for talk at evenings of the events of the day; for the ecstasy of caresses; for gay mockery at each other's follies; for plans and projects, fun and struggle; praying that we may neither neglect nor undervalue these things, nor be tempted to think of them as self-contained and self-sufficient.

*London Yearly Meeting, 1960*

These six sayings are basically all the important messages
that one person can give to another.
I love you.
Thank you.
I'm sorry.
I need help.
That's not good enough.
No.

*John Calvi, 1988*

We are called to obedient love
even though we may not
be feeling very loving.
Often it is through
the performance of loving acts
that loving feelings can be built up in us.
We may start with small,
perhaps very tiny steps.

*Sandra Cronk, 1983*

It [simplicity] is about mending and
caring for things rather than discarding
them at the first sign of age or wear and
the uplifting implications this ethic
has on personal relationships.
 It's about . . . working to make commitments
rather than to guard options.

*Frank Levering and Wanda Urbanska, 1992*


If I am very aware that I do not love much,
the way is not to try to love more,
so much as to spend more time
in trying to open myself
to receive the love of God.

*Damaris. Parker-Rhodes, 1985*


It is in the field of personal relations that fear reveals its most sinister characteristic. It tends to create what we are afraid of. Any intimate relationship with another person depends on mutual trust. If I fear to lose the relationship, I have already diminished the trust. If I go on the defensive for fear of losing my friend; if I do something to prevent what I fear, then I poison the friendship and make its loss more likely. What we seek in friendship and love is to be wholly ourselves, in equality and freedom, with another person. And there is nothing we can do about this except to trust, to have faith, and to set our friend free of us.

*John Macmurray, 1964*


Out of fear we may betray truth;
out of bitterness or self-righteousness
we may betray love.

*Margarethe Lachmund, 1953*


We have to forgive each other,
not for what we have done,

but for what we are.
For being so infinitely less
than we ought to be.
We have to learn to give
where we had hoped to get
and to understand where
we had hoped to be understood.

*Harold Loukes, 1958*


Two young trees are planted close together
in common soil at marriage.
They send down roots together,
and feed on many of these same nutrients.
But as they grow taller and older
some of the roots shoot out in different directions,
away from each other, seeking mutually alien soil.
Nevertheless, the older original roots stay intertwined.
The trees also grow above ground.
Many of their branches intertwine and
shape each other in the happy embrace of shared space. . . .
But these trees are not only growing toward each other;
they are growing in all directions.
Like the roots, some of the branches
stretch far away from the common center,
and breathe a mutually alien air.
Each tree is in itself whole and individual
and growing according to its inner design,
yet shaped on the one side by its partner,
and on the other by the outside world.

*Elise Boulding, 1989*


We wish those getting married a lifetime of happiness together,
but few lives are full of joy. Sorrow and pain come to all of us.
Problems can divide us, or we can grow together through them.
Facing economic reverses, disasters, serious illness, and death
honestly and supportively can strengthen a relationship. Much of

life consists, however, of going on day after day, without making much visible progress, doing our work as faithfully as we can, with no special reward or recognition. Our mate's understanding of the need for encouragement, of a break—sometimes in the form of a special treat or gift or night out—can make an enormous difference. If, however, we expect our mates to support us in idleness or carry a disproportionate share of the load or smooth out all our difficulties and shield us from disaster, we are doomed to disappointment. No marriage can grow into wholeness unless both work at it with mutual forbearance and trust and caring.

*Elizabeth Watson, 1981*

If truth be told,
It was not priest, who made us one,
Nor finger
circled with gold,
Nor soft delights when day is done
and arms enfold.
These bonds are firm,
but in death-storm
They may not hold—
We were welded man and wife
By hammer-strokes of daily life.

*Ellen Sophia Bosanquet, 1938*

Since God is the author of love, no couple can without God make good their promise to love one another for the rest of their lives. . . . Love must inevitably change and mature, and every relationship has its times of stress as well as its times of renewal. But there are periods in some married lives when all that can be done is to go on trying to love and to continue to believe in the elusive and unique quality for which we gave ourselves to our partner until death should part us. . . .

What a triumph when old love is transformed into deeper, surer new love which can accept more fully what each has, and the pair find a rebirth together in those things which are eternal, and through this a renewal of their everyday living.

*London Yearly Meeting, 1959*

. . . There always seems to be enough love to deal with even the most enormous hurt or conflict between us. We have tested this reluctantly, unintentionally, and found, to our great relief, that life apart is out of the question. The question is always—what are we going to do with this obstacle? And, like all other traumas, if we can use it for learning, then we can turn pain into wisdom. But it means doing the homework—reaching, changing, and going to new ground without maps. Sometimes I wonder if this is why so many marriages fail. Where in life do we have any preparation to be shown our worst selves by someone who loves us and understands it as a gift to become better at being who we are?

*John Calvi, 1997*

In the true marriage relationship
the independence of husband and wife is equal,
their dependence mutual,
and their obligations reciprocal.

*Lucretia Mott, 1850*

Do we not have, in marriage,
a powerful opportunity to demonstrate
in one nuclear human relationship
all we stand for, and
all we seek to proclaim to the wider world?

*David R. Mace, 1969*

QUERIES

🙠 Do I easily say: "I love you. Thank you. I'm sorry. I need help. That's not good enough. No"?

🙠 Am I prepared to be shown my worst self by someone who loves me, and to understand his or her constructive criticism as a gift to help me become a better person, better at being who I really am?

🙠 Do I seek to make my partnership or marriage reflect my faith and the values I aspire to stand for in the wider world?

Something of God
comes into our world
with every child that is born.
There is here with the newborn child
a divine spark, a light within. . . .

*Rufus M. Jones, 1948*

I was not "christened" in a church, but I was sprinkled from morning to night with the dew of religion. We never ate a meal together which did not begin with a hush of thanksgiving; we never began a day without a "family gathering," at which my mother read a chapter of the Bible, after which there would follow a weighty silence. . . . My first steps in religion were thus acted. It was a religion we did together. Almost nothing was said in the way of instructing me. We all joined together to listen for God and then one of us talked to God for the others. In these simple ways my religious disposition was being unconsciously formed. . . .

*Rufus M. Jones, 1926*

Children are far more mystical-minded than their elders suspect, and mystics would not be so rare if we made better use of the culture of silence in the lives of our children.

*Rufus M. Jones, 1928*

. . . It is possible to drown children and adults in a constant flow of stimuli, forcing them to spend so much energy responding to the outside world that inward life and the creative imagination which flowers from it becomes stunted or atrophied.

. . . In homes where silence is lived, the child finds it easy and comfortable to turn to it. In a large and noisy family (like my own) the period of hush that begins every meal sweeps like a healing wind over all the cross-currents that have built up in the previous hours and leaves the household clean and sweet. Times apart of special family worship, hard to come by in the daily routine, become hours to be remembered and valued for their very scarcity, and never fail to catch us up to another level of love and awareness. In these times we rediscover who and what we really are, as individuals and as a family, and can lay before God what we cannot easily lay before one another. It is an odd thing to say, but solitude can be shared. In a family where inward solitude is highly prized, individuals may slip easily into and out of each other's solitude. Some families must work harder than others to create the physical situation in which times of solitude become possible, but when silence is treasured, the quiet place is found.

*Elise Boulding, 1962*

Becoming educated is the only process that engages every human being every day of his or her life. School, as adults come to realize, is only the beginning of learning. What many parents overlook is that education is an all-day and every-day event that begins and ends at home. Longfellow wrote, "A single conversation across the table with a wise person is better than ten years' mere study of books." As often as not that "conversation across a table" takes place during a family's breakfast or dinner, and that "wise person" is usually a father or a mother. Parents are every child's first teachers, and any school, no matter how good, can only build on those first, most formative lessons.

*Robert Lawrence Smith, 1998*

Teachers are optimists. We would not be teachers if we did not have confidence in the future and in humankind. We trust that given the right opportunities children will grow up into responsible adults capable of making good choices and of saving the world from disaster. Perhaps the most important thing we can do today is to transmit to our pupils that sense of hope. . . . The two qualities which are most important to children of today are hope and imagination. Hope to believe they can change the world they live in and imagination to find ways to do so.

*Janet Gilbraith, 1986*

. . . Finally and painfully
I came to the conclusion
that in a family
we are one another's destiny
both for good and ill.
We too had parents and
they had parents—
and parenting is chancy.
Try as hard as one can,
still one makes nearly fatal mistakes.

*Damaris Parker-Rhodes, 1985*


After endeavoring to do the best we can
in providing for education, and placing them out,
we must leave our children to the Lord
and their own conduct, as after all our labors,
and with the Divine blessing upon these labors,
they may if they will, as some unhappily do,
forsake their own mercies,
and pursue a wrong course. . . .
So . . . commending them to the care of
Israel's unslumbering shepherd,
there to their own determination
we must finally leave them.

*Jonathan Hutchinson, 1825*


Our belief in the divine spark
in each individual person involve[s]
complete respect for the soul of a child:
they belong to themselves
even before they belong to their parents,
from whom they are often different
in temperament, tastes, and abilities.

*France Yearly Meeting, 1963*

Children have much to teach us. If we cultivated the habit of dialogue and mutual learning, our children could keep us growing, and in a measure could bring us into their future. . . .

*Elizabeth Watson, 1975*

QUERIES

- Do I honor children's need for quiet times, and do I work to create situations where solitude for children becomes possible?

- After endeavoring to do my best as a parent, do I remember with humility that parenting is difficult and chancy, and that I must forgive myself for making mistakes?

- Do I convey a sense of hopefulness to the children in my life, and do I foster in them the imagination and confidence that they can change the world?

As wisdom dawns with age,
we begin to measure our experiences
not by what life gives to us,
not by the things withheld from us,
but by their power to help us
to grow in spiritual wisdom.

*Evelyn Sturge, 1949*

The whole point of living is to become spiritually aware
in thinking, feeling, suffering, and doing.
It is not success so much that matters any more,
as becoming more deeply human—
that is kinder, truer, more to be relied on
and less automatic in response.

*Damaris Parker-Rhodes, 1985*

What Life Has Taught Me:
Resentment is poisonous;
Compassion is healing;
Love is creative.

*Ellen Sophia Bosanquet, 1960*

I am convinced it is a great art to know how to grow old gracefully, and I am determined to practice it. . . . I always thought I should love to grow old, and I find it is even more delightful than I thought. It is so delicious to be done with things, and to feel no need any longer to concern myself much about earthly affairs. . . . I am tremendously content to let one activity after another go, and to await quietly and happily the opening of the door at the end of the passage way, that will let me in to my real abiding place.

*Hannah Whitall Smith, 1903*

The first fifty years of my life were very energetic. With a New England missionary father and a mother also from a minister's family, we were brought up to be good, waste not a minute, work hard, perform tasks that you could check off your list or put in your diary as finished. Later we were expected to do good with work that would bring about desirable social changes. . . . It wasn't until I was fifty-five that this strenuous performance was broken. As I moved from doing good, to being good, I finally came to understand it was all right for me to simply be.

*Mary Millman, 1992*

I have been thinking over my life and the survey has not been encouraging. Alas! If I have been a servant at all, I have been an unprofitable one. And yet I have loved goodness and longed to be good, but it has been so hard to bring my imaginative, poetic temperament into subjection. I stand ashamed and almost despairing before holy and pure ideals. As I read the New Testament I feel how weak, irresolute, and frail I am and how little I can rely on anything save Our Lord's mercy, and infinite compassion, which I reverently and thoughtfully own have followed me through life, and the assurance of which is my sole ground of hope for myself and for those I love and pray for.

*John Greenleaf Whittier, 1880*

I do believe that old age can cause unknown inner transubstantiation, and the diminishments may be taken as the test of "God the amazing Guru." It is the fiery tests of life that can cause pieces of our inner mechanism to begin functioning for the first time; tests that turn into Initiations. . . . There is a difference between accepting fate and wrestling with it so that it may yield up spiritual fruit. One does not know if one will be strong enough so to wrestle, but "God's strength is made perfect in weakness." There is no doubt that if I am to change and mature and at the end look back on a fulfilled life, the process of becoming has to continue until the last.

*Damaris Parker-Rhodes, 1985*

As one grows older and more devastating diminishments are
undergone, if these deprivations, losses, and limitations can be
hallowed, it is possible to become ever more sensitive to, and
more perceptive of, meaningful coincidence. It is natural to struggle against diminishments, like Jacob wrestling with the angel. It
is well to see that, in doing so, one is struggling against an angel
and not to let go until one has received the distinctive blessing of
that particular angel. Even if one goes away limping badly, the
diminishment will have been hallowed by this blessing.

*John Yungblut, 1990*

There are simple ways in which it is possible to prepare the body
and mind for the spirit's release into the larger world beyond
death. Learning to say goodbye to outworn roles starts back in
middle age. As parents we have to see our children grow up and
depart into the world. Retirement takes away a lifetime's occupations, and the body gradually becomes unable to be so
active. . . . Each deprivation then may be found to be the necessary stripping undertaken by the mountain-climber who, at every
hut on his journey into the higher altitudes, finds a depot for
what must be left behind.

*Damaris Parker-Rhodes, 1985*

Henry Cadbury in his late eighties had two wishes:
not to live too long, and to live long enough.

*Elizabeth Gray Vining, 1979*

Age comes, and without jobs, without the energy to fill all our
hours with activity, with decreased ability to read, to travel, and
sometimes even to knit, we have much more time to think. We
lie awake for hours at night. And we find, some of us, that what
we thought was faith was not much more than well-being, that
our realization of God and God's love was academic, unreal,
unconvincing. The words used so easily by spiritual writers and
the devout seem empty and perfunctory. The little books on our
bedside tables have been read and re-read until all the juice has
gone out of them. What now?

Consider thy old friends, O God, whose years are increasing. Provide for them homes of dignity and freedom. Give them, in case of need, understanding helpers and the willingness to accept help. Deepen their joy in the beauty of thy world and their love for their neighbors, grant them courage in the face of pain or weakness, and always a sure knowledge of thy presence.

*Elizabeth Gray Vining, 1982*

QUERIES

& *How has aging changed my awareness of God's presence in my life?*

& *As I age do I cultivate the gifts of kindness, acceptance, and deepened spiritual awareness?*

& *Do I accept my diminishments and seek to find in them a blessing?*

When my mother-in-law was a young woman, she came to the point of not understanding why her family was so interested in attending church. She could not see the use in religion, and decided that she would no longer believe in God. However, the day came when she found herself sitting on the back steps looking up into a magnificent fall sky and was overwhelmed by the beauty that surrounded her. Suddenly she realized she couldn't give up God because "then there would be no one to thank."

*Barbara Cummings St. John, 1995*

All our senses are given to us to enjoy,
and to praise God.
The smell of the sea,
the blossom borne on the wind,
of the soft flesh of a little baby;
the taste of a ripe plum
or bread fresh from the oven,
the feel of warm cat's fur,
or the body of a lover—
these are all forms of thanksgiving prayer.

*Bella Bown, 1980*

When you want very much
something that you can have
consider it a gift;
accept it gracefully.

*Becky Birtha, 1991*

. . . Joy came in the morning . . .
and the storms in measure over,
and the spring time came,
and the singing of birds,
and the voice of the Turtle is heard in our land.
O! the glorious day that is dawned upon us,

where the morning stars do sing together,
and all the sons and daughters of God
do shout for joy. . . .
Oh God's tender dealings can never
be erased from our remembering,
for God has printed them in our hearts. . . .

*Katherine Whitton, 1681*


Something seen, something heard, something felt, flashes upon one with a bright freshness, and the heart, tired or sick or sad or merely indifferent, stirs and lifts in answer. Different things do it for different people, but the result is the same: that fleeting instant when we lose ourselves in joy and wonder. It is minor because it is slight and so soon gone; it is an ecstasy because there is an impersonal quality in the vivid thrust of happiness we feel, and because the stir lingers in the memory.

*Elizabeth Gray Vining, 1942*


Who has never felt melted down and brought to tears of tenderness at a great passage in a book, a scene in a play, a sight of the sea, a word or the hug of a child, a surge of pain, a midnight hour in a "white night" when we have been shown the way and have yielded, or at one of those moments in a conversation with a friend where we touched "where words come from"? These minor ecstasies, as Elizabeth Vining calls them, are all fingers. They all point to the Presence.

*Douglas V. Steere, 1967*


There is a particular kind of Quaker humor that is gentle and dry and we chuckle when we are privy to it. . . . It is a humor that has the universal appeal of holding up the mirror for us to unthreateningly see ourselves and the human condition in wonderful clarity. Thank God for the grace of humor, without which we would be less than human and less aware of the signals of transcendence within ourselves and others.

*William O. Brown, 1978*

We can laugh with rather than laugh at. We can puncture pomposity while recognizing our propensity to pride. We can chuckle at the foibles and failures of others, yet do it with a spirit that acknowledges them as our foibles as well. Surely a people that refuses guns for Jesus' sake should measure carefully the firepower of their jokes. Compassionate humor embraces more than it embarrasses. As we laugh arm-in-arm, we can go forward together in all our human weakness and human possibility.

*Howard Macy, 1993*

As the plow turns over the earth and prepares it to receive the seed, so humor exposes the undetected inadequacies and contradictions of our assumptions. Humor makes us receptive to the convicting power of truth.

*Paul Anderson, 1993*

When we are, however, able to accept being accepted, able to receive the loving, listening presence of God both embodied in others and hidden in their hearts, we experience God as love. The experience of such love results spontaneously in gratitude, praise, and joy. This is not the "duty of being grateful" I'm speaking of. I mean an upwelling of heart-breaking, heart-opening thankfulness, and joy that such love could be, that we could be in it, that it could be in us, that we are all in it together.

*Patricia Loring, 1997*

Sing and rejoice you children
of the day and of the Light.
For the Lord is at work
in this thick night of darkness that [may] be felt.
Truth does flourish as the rose,
the lilies do grow among the thorns,
the plants a-top of the hills,
and upon them the lambs do skip and play.

*George Fox, 1663*

QUERIES

&⸒ Am I a grateful recipient of the gifts that life provides? How do I express my gratitude?

&⸒ Do I live with a grace and lightness that make joy and laughter part of my everyday life?

&⸒ Do I live expectantly, watching and listening for life's "minor ecstasies"?

# CHAPTER 4

Unexpected Songs

for Times of

Fear

Suffering

Despair

Death

Grief

Hope

When things fall apart, fear creeps in, despair fills our souls, and we ask ourselves and God, "Why me?" It is hard to trust and difficult to pray to the One we are questioning: "Why is there pain and why do the innocent suffer?" When it is midnight in our soul, we feel totally alone, unable to make meaning of life, and shut off from the Comforter. The sound of desolation fills our ears, and it is hard to hear the singing that heralds the break of day.

Barbara Cummings St. John recounts a story about her mother who was taking care of a four-year-old boy whose parents were in England. One afternoon, the child climbed to the top of a very tall maple tree and was too frightened to come down or even to call for help. Barbara's mother looked out the window, saw the child paralyzed by fear, and was not sure how to respond. She gathered herself and then calmly walked outside, looked up at the terrified child high in the tree, and said, "If I were a little bird up there, I would sing a little song." Turning away, she slowly walked back into the house so that he would not feel her fear. After a few minutes of watching him from behind a curtain, she heard his small voice tentatively begin a wavering little song as he started to slowly climb down the tree. Barbara's reflection is that there may not always be an answer to fear and isolation, but there is always a song.[10]

In those times of midnight in our soul, when despair overtakes our memories of blessings past, it is hard to believe that "a new song will be put in our mouths."[11] It is then, listening beyond our desolation, that we can sometimes hear the Eternal Guide who sings a song of hope in the middle of the night.

In the economy of the Spirit nothing is ever wasted. When the hard ground of our heart is broken open by suffering, over time new possibilities for faithful plain living may emerge. This chapter is about experiencing difficult times, hearing unexpected songs, and growing into new possibilities.

Christ's major point
throughout the Sermon on the Mount
is to get rid of fears and anxieties.
It might almost be said that
the substance of his mission
as a teacher was to
set us free from the slavery of fears.
"Why are ye so fearful?"
he keeps saying.
Stop your unnecessary worries.
Cut out your excessive anxieties.
It has been well said that
the most ruinously expensive
of all our emotions is fear.
It is that very emotion of fear
that has thrown our world out of joint
and brought us to this unspeakable calamity. . . .

*Rufus M. Jones, written between
1939 and 1942*

What would I do if I were not afraid?

*Martha E. Manglesdorf, 1994*

The Hebrew slaves had imagined that freedom from physical captivity would allow them to live as free people. But they discovered that they had brought their slavery with them. They were enslaved to fear. . . .

The wilderness wandering, this season of repeated failure and renewed stripping, was their time of learning. . . . In the wilderness the people recognized that their food came from God. Their drink came from God. Their very survival came from God. Only as they gave up reliance on their own power did they come to trust God's faithful leading. Paradoxically, it was this detachment from their own power which made them strong enough to enter the Promised Land.

*Sandra Cronk, 1991*

Through prayer we must also eradicate fear—of making fools of ourselves, of making mistakes, of being hurt; fear creates the very things we dread. It is a plague. It comes from lack of love. . . . And the psalmist sang, "The Lord is my light and my salvation; whom shall I fear? The Lord is the strength of my life; of whom shall I be afraid?"

*Adam Curle, 1981*

In fear of our emotions,
we have lost our hearts.
We are now at a state of
being without love.
The heart is withered
and is dying.

*Louise Wilson, 1994*

. . . [W]hat is characteristic of human beings is that we do not live in the moment. We look before and after. We carry our past experience with us and project it on the future. And if the past has frightened us, we carry that with us and project it ahead. . . . I wonder if you ever catch yourself, as I do sometimes, feeling anxious, and looking for something to be anxious about? But mostly we don't catch these fears at work. They have become habits and we are quite unaware of them. . . .

The person who is fear-determined is always on the defensive. You will recognize these people when you meet them because either they hide from you behind a facade of pretense or formality, or else they try to dominate you. They are either submissive or aggressive. . . . They can never be themselves. They have lost their freedom; and losing their freedom they have lost their lives.

*John Macmurray, 1964*

I chose to attend a weekend course at Hurricane Island, off the coast of Maine. In the middle of that week, I faced the challenge I feared most. One of our instructors backed me up to the edge of a cliff 110 feet above solid ground. He tied a very thin rope to my waist—a rope that looked ill-kempt to me and seemed to be starting to unravel—and told me to start "rappelling" down that cliff. "Do what?" I said. "Just go!" the instructor explained. So I went—and immediately slammed into a ledge, some four feet down from the edge of the cliff, with bone-jarring, brain-jarring force. The instructor looked down at me: "I don't think you've quite got it." "Right," said I. . . . So I tried it again, my way—and slammed into the next ledge, another four feet down. "You still don't have it," the instructor said helpfully.

I was about halfway down when the second instructor called up from below: "Parker, I think you'd better stop and see what's just below your feet." I lowered my eyes very slowly—so as not to shift my weight—and saw that I was approaching a deep hole in the face of the rock. I froze, paralyzed with fear.

The second instructor let me hang there, trembling, in silence, for what seemed like a very long time. Finally, she shouted up these helpful words: "Parker, is anything wrong?" To this day, I do not know where my words came from, though I have twelve witnesses to the fact that I spoke them. In a high, squeaky voice, I said, "I don't want to talk about it." "Then," said the second instructor, "it's time that you learned the Outward Bound motto." "If you can't get out of it, get into it!"

. . . There was no way out of my dilemma except to get into it—so my feet started to move, and . . . I made it safely down.

*Parker J. Palmer, 2000*

My job was to be eliminated, and soon I would be unemployed. My mood darkened to match the night outside. . . . Twenty-five years later I still do not know where the words came from, but I recall writing them down on a paper napkin: "Without fear there could be no courage. Without courage there would be no hope. And without hope, life would not be worth living."

Until that moment, I had never thought of myself as a courageous person. In fact, most of my thoughts about courage had focused on the times my courage had failed. But now I had glimpsed a mysterious relationship between fear and courage that I had never considered before. . . . For the first time in my life, I began to accept my fears as a natural part of living instead of trying to eliminate them by being perfectly courageous all the time. I was beginning to see courage and fear as "dancing partners" rather than either/or opposites.

*Lyman Randall, 1999*

Let our faith free us from crippling fears
so that we may live adventurously.

*New England Yearly Meeting of Friends, 1985*

QUERIES

- *What would I do if I were not afraid?*

- *What are the unnecessary fears and excessive anxieties that sometimes create the very things I dread?*

- *Do I accept my fears as a natural part of living, and look for ways they may invite me to be courageous?*

During many nights in recent years and many mornings
when I awake, I have felt like building an altar,
for I did not believe that I could have felt
this much pain and survived.
But I have. There is resurrection.
I know that when I lose the capacity to feel,
when I cannot feel my foot or my hand,
I feel dead inside; I feel alone, unconnected.
When I begin to feel any feeling again,
it is a resurrection, a return to life.
I know experientially that to heal
is an increased capacity to feel.
And we can only feel incredibly grateful
when we perceive again that
vibrant Life that is the center of everything.

*Janet Hoffman, 1990*

Following the operation all sense of God disappeared, and anyone who came to my bedside . . . I asked to take my hand and
mediate God's love to me. In fact healing and prayer surrounded
me on every hand, although I myself felt cut off in complete
inner aridity except when actually held in the inner place by
someone taking my hand and praying.

*Damaris Parker-Rhodes, 1985*

Don't be deceived. You must face Destiny.
Preparation is only possible now.
Don't be fooled by your sunny skies.
When the rains descend and the floods come
and the winds blow and beat upon your house,
your private dwelling, your own family,
your own fair hopes, your own strong muscles,
your own body, your own soul itself,
then it is well-nigh too late to build a house.

You can only go inside what house you have
and pray that it is founded upon the Rock.
Be not deceived by distance in time or space,
or the false security of a bank account
and an automobile and good health
and willing hands to work.
Thousands, perhaps millions as good as you
have had all these things
and are perishing in body and, worse still, in soul today.

For if you accept as normal life
only what you can understand,
then you will only try to expel
the dull, dead weight of Destiny,
of inevitable suffering which is a part of normal life,
and never come to terms with it
or fit your soul to the collar
and bear the burden of your suffering
which must be borne by you,
or enter into the divine education and drastic discipline of
        sorrow,
or rise radiant in the sacrament of pain.

*Thomas R. Kelly, 1939*

Out of our brokenness make us a blessing. . . .

*Judith L. Brutz, 1990*

God does not shelter us from misfortune,
but God does help us to endure it,
and so suffering above all else
can become the point of encounter with God.

*Diana Lampen, 1996*

Now that suffering is upon the world
we cannot appeal to
the escalator theory of suffering

and expect that suffering will inevitably
shake great souls into life.
No, there is nothing about suffering
such that it automatically purges
the dross from human nature and
brings heroic souls upon the scene.
Suffering can blast and blight
an earnest but unprepared soul,
and damn it utterly to despair.
No, only those who go
into the travail of today,
bearing a seed within them,
a seed of awareness
of the heavenly dimensions of humanity,
can return in joy.

*Thomas R. Kelly, 1939*

We can choose to use our own pain
to affirm our solidarity with humanity,
and we can transform
some of the evil with love.

*Ann Barclay, 1978*

For many months she had fought tenaciously against the
remorseless strokes of a rare and inevitably fatal disease, an afflic-
tion that seemed so senseless, so wasteful of a noble spirit, as to
evoke all human doubts about a beneficent providence. In a weak
moment I remarked to her, "Isn't it strange that this should have
happened to us?" She looked at me in surprise and said, "But if
it happens, why shouldn't it happen to us?"

For the first time in my life the full meaning of the Cross was
given to me. I found myself confronted with that finest essence
of the imagination which unselfconsciously and willingly shared
pain with all mankind. I saw the Cross, the Cross of Jesus and
cross of humanity, as the final service of love, pain as the final
sharing of love, the final argument that has no roots in logic,

carrying its winged appeal beyond all reason and philosophy.

I saw here the humble human person sharing in the pain of humankind and in the divine pain and sacrifice that Christ shares with us. And I realized that there are some ways of dealing with pain that transform the sufferer into a socially creative person. Thus we are left with no resentment, only with a deep thankfulness that flows over grief and deprivation, all self-pity and regret obliterated by the final victory.

*Edgar B. Castle, 1961*

"Nothing matters; everything matters."
It is a key of entrance into suffering.
He who knows only one-half of the paradox
can never enter that door of mystery and survive.

*Thomas R. Kelly, 1939*

When people have to go through really deep sorrow, when something of the fundamentals of their lives is destroyed, they feel as if they walk and live under a great glass bowl. They see and hear other people, but they seem separated from them by an intense pain that others, even the most sympathetic, cannot feel. But if love works its great miracle, it reaches through the invisible wall. You do not forget what you lost, but sometimes you think that now for the first time you feel the innermost reality and beauty of joy, the creative power which comes to you out of it. . . . Suffering and joy are in a miraculous way connected with each other in this world of God.

*Emil Fuchs, 1949*

The uses we make of sorrow
are the measure of our spiritual growth.

*Diana Lampen, 1996*

This is a healing poem
For when you cannot dance
and cannot work
and cannot walk.
Concentrate on
the things you still can do.
Breathe.
Dream.
Love.
Change.

*Becky Birtha, 1991*

QUERIES

℞ *Am I cultivating a discipline of spiritual awareness that will help me withstand the blasts and blights of personal suffering?*

℞ *In the midst of suffering do I look vigilantly for points of encounter with God?*

℞ *What have I learned from the suffering in my life, and how am I using what I have learned?*

The whys are endless. I think we are meant to ask them. To fail to ask, to accept mindlessly the dark side of the human condition, is to seek to numb ourselves to reality. And—because we cannot numb one dimension of our feelings in isolation from the rest— as we shut out our own pain, we foreclose the possibility of compassion for others who suffer, we foreclose the impetus for the prophetic word to the unjust and—worst of all—we risk becoming part of the darkness even as we accept it.

*Patricia Loring, 1997*

We shall not find the explanation on the level of justice.
To seek it on this level is to face defeat,
for justice is not the supreme good.
Christian doctrine offers a way out beyond justice,
pointing not to the solution of a mystery
but to the painful conquest of the inevitable.
Nothing in the Gospels explains pain or evil;
Christ showed us how to meet the challenge.
And that is all. Briefly, then, we may say that
the problem of pain and evil can be solved up to a point
but that from this point there remains only a challenge
which we face with an act of faith and will,
or refuse to face.

*Edgar B. Castle, 1961*

The first lesson is where everyone starts:
despair that clears the way. . . .
Despair shouldn't be cultivated,
just allowed to surface.
Being useless uncovers despair,
and the same empowerment occurs
when the optimist ceases to grasp at the future,
when the mourner ceases to grasp at the past, or
when the bereft ceases to grasp at what might have been.

*Jim Corbett, 1991*

. . . Real despair comes from clinging to the conviction that if I cannot "make meaning" for my life—by making money, friends, changes—there is no meaning to life at all. True despair is the refusal to recognize the fragility of all our efforts at making [meaning], the ease with which our making is destroyed by error, evil, illness, age, death. The joy beyond despair comes when we abandon the exhausting illusion of self-sufficiency and become the grateful recipients of the gifts that life provides.

*Parker J. Palmer, 1990*


Those who have traveled in the dark night
have both very daring and, at the same time,
very practical advice to give to new journeyers.
"Stay in the darkness and emptiness.
Do not flee from the nothingness or
try to fill up that hollow place
with your own attempts to create new finite pillars
on which to build your life." . . .
In the darkness, all reliance on our human efforts
to bring salvation is shattered.
The old self dies. Into emptiness God brings new life.

*Sandra Cronk, 1991*


Friends, whatever ye are addicted to,
the tempter will come in that thing;
and when it can trouble you,
then it gets advantage over you,
and then you are gone.
Stand still in that which is pure,
after ye see yourselves; and then mercy comes in.
After thou seest thy thoughts,
and the temptations, do not think, but submit;
and then power comes.
Stand still in that which shows and discovers;
and then doth strength immediately come.
And stand still in the Light, and submit to it, and

the other will be hush'd and gone;
and then content comes.

*George Fox, 1698*


The extent of human loneliness is beyond imagining.
We all have to cope with it,
and no one can fully relieve us of it. . . .

*Diana Lampen, 1996*


Oh the grief and distress of my poor soul!
The divine presence was withdrawn,
and I had no friend on earth to speak to.

*Catherine Phillips, 1797*


The loneliness thou speaks of I know. For do not think, darling, that it is confined to unmarried people. It is just as real in lives that have plenty of human ties, husbands, and children, and friends. It is the loneliness of this world life, the loneliness of hearts that are made for union with God, but which have not yet fully realized it. I believe it is inseparable from humanity. I believe God has ordained it in the very nature of things by creating us for God's self alone. . . . Thee will accept it as a God-given blessing meant only to drive thee to God. Thy loneliness is only different in kind but not in fact from the loneliness of every human heart apart from God. Thy circumstances are lonely, but thy loneliness of spirit does not come from these, it is the loneliness of humanity. Therefore, nothing but God can satisfy it.

*Hannah Whitall Smith, 1882*


I bow my forehead to the dust,
I veil mine eyes for shame,
And urge, in trembling self-distrust,
A prayer without a claim.

I see the wrong that round me lies,
I feel the guilt within. . . .

Yet, in the maddening maze of things
And tossed by storm and flood,
To one fixed trust my spirit clings;
I know that God is good.

*John Greenleaf Whittier, 1865*

"As a parent, the Lord pities us. For God knows our frame; God remembers that we are dust" (Psalm 103). If Yahweh remembers that we are dust, that growth costs, that we need each other, that even when we are strong we are also vulnerable—can we remember, can we remember . . . ?

*Sharon Daloz Parks, 1986*

QUERIES

- *Do I allow my despair to surface? Do I avoid cultivating despair?*

- *During times of despair do I stay present to the feeling of emptiness and wait for God to fill it with new life?*

- *When I am in despair what tempts me? Do I ask for divine assistance in resisting my temptation?*

The truest end of life is to know
the Life that never ends. . . .
For though death be a dark passage,
it leads to immortality. . . .

For death is no more than a
Turning of us over from time to eternity.
Death then, being the way and condition of life,
we cannot love to live,
if we cannot bear to die. . . .

*William Penn, 1693*

Oh God, spirit of the universe, I am old in years and in the sight of others, but I do not feel old within myself. I have hopes and purposes, things I wish to do before I die. A surging of life within me cries, "Not yet, not yet," more strongly than it did ten years ago, perhaps because the nearer approach of death arouses a defensive strength of the instinct to cling to life. Help me to loosen fiber by fiber the instinctive strings that bind me to the life I know. Infuse me with Thy spirit so that it is Thee I turn to, not the old ropes of habit and thought. . . .

Keep me ever aware and ever prepared for the summons. If pain comes before the end, help me not to fear it or struggle against it but to welcome it as a hastening of the process by which the strings that bind me to life are untied. Give me joy in awaiting the great change that comes after this life of many changes, grant that my self be merged in Thy self as a candle's wavering light is caught up into the sun.

*Elizabeth Gray Vining, 1979*

It's not death that scares me so much
as not living as fully as I can.

*Lori Barg, 1998*

One woman told me she did not fear death itself at all; but she did very much fear the process of dying, and was particularly worried as to how she might behave towards the end. She had seen so many people become difficult and cantankerous, and feared she might do the same. How easy it is to share this fear of hers! Maybe the last act of humility required of us is that we accept and love ourselves to the end, however we may be by then. Learning to accept and forgive ourselves is such an important step towards becoming whole. When Jesus said, "Love your neighbor as yourself," he did not mean for us to concentrate on the first three words. He knew that loving ourselves is a prerequisite of loving anyone else. When a much-loved member of our Quaker Meeting became very distressed and querulous in her dying weeks, she was not rejected by us. It seemed we loved her more than ever. We find it so hard to extend this same sort of love to ourselves in our own frailties.

*Diana Lampen, 1996*

While I was undergoing chemotherapy and radiation treatments for Hodgkin's Lymphoma, my "quality of life," by most of the usual standards, would have been considered very low. I was in real pain or extreme discomfort most of the time for many months, suffering from nerve damage, nausea, muscle cramps, mouth sores, headaches, and severe radiation burns on my skin, throat, and esophagus. Eating and sleeping were a struggle rather than a pleasure. My thought processes were slowed and sometimes distorted, my memory weakened, my concentration limited. . . . I communicated less and less, as I focused my energies on inner experiences I could not describe with words. . . .

The difficulties were real, the pain was real, the stripping away of identity was very real—yet the opportunity for a new understanding of myself and of God was still more real, pervasive, and palpable during this time. When all the usual standards for a "good life" were gone, other standards emerged. I found that without the things that had superficially defined my life, I still had a life, and one that was filled with richness, wonder, beauty, a kind of grace. It was incredible to discover that my deeper identity—my capacity to feel love and experience joy, my awareness of being part of something larger and more meaningful—

did not depend upon physical comfort, the ability to do things in the world, or even the ability to think about things in a particular, familiar way. I was still myself even as my body and my everyday life went to pieces. And I am quite sure that I will still be myself when my body and everyday life ultimately fall away completely as I prepare for death.

*Kirsten Backstrom, 1998*

Death rims life with the beauty of Transiency. It is because beauty is always passing—clouds moving, waters flowing, leaves scattering, youth aging—that it so pierces our hearts.

*Bradford Smith, 1965*

That death seems but a covered way
Which opens into light,
Wherein no blinded child can stray
Beyond God's loving sight. . . .

And so the shadows fall apart,
And so the west winds play;
And all the windows of my heart
I open to the day.

*John Greenleaf Whittier, 1856*

Whittier's own death was a beautiful one. He was eighty-four. He was staying with a friend in Hampton Falls, New Hampshire, when he suffered a stroke. For the three days that he lived, he was full of acceptance. "It is all right. Everybody is so kind." And of love; over and over he said, "Love, love to all the world." On September 6 as the sun was rising, he died.

*Elizabeth Gray Vining, 1979*

The time is at hand wherein time shall be no more;
and then whatever had a being in time,
shall cease from being so any longer.
We must all look to the grave, to the dust;

we must all sleep an eternal sleep,
when once the last night comes:
when we shall bury all our quarrels and contentions,
and awake in perfect life and love: and then we shall be,
both to ourselves and one another,
what now we cannot so much as desire to be.

*Isaac Penington, 1650*


If you think about it, there are no boundaries between one organism and another, between "life" and "non-life." We are constantly flowing from one to another: One moment a skin cell is a portion of a human being, the next moment it is part of a dust pile; then it is transformed into a house plant or a rhododendron bush; then it becomes oxygen to be breathed in by a possum, whose wastes feed bacteria that bring nutrients to an oak tree, which feeds a gypsy moth. All through the food web and non-living world we travel, zillions of fragments are forever being put together and taken apart to make yet more unique creations. Physically we possess no true boundaries; we are forever re-molded and recast into new forms.

Francis Hole, a soil scientist and poet (and Friend), has said, "Our bodies are disposable, biodegradable containers for spirit." We are worms and granite, oak trees and robins, sea spume and mica; we are stardust . . . we are each as old as the universe.

*Lisa Lofland Gould, 1999*


And so comes the next opening—the sense of being part of a universe, a personal relatedness to all life, all growth, all creativity. Suddenly one senses that this life is not just our own little individual existence, that we are bound in fact to all of life, from the first splitting off of the planets, through the beginning of animate life, and on through the slow evolution of humanity. It is all in us and we are but one channel of it. What has flowed through us, flows on, through children, through works accomplished, through services rendered; it is not lost. Once given the vision of one's true place in the life stream, death is no longer complete or final, but an incident. Death is the way—the only way—life renews itself. When the individual has served their purpose as a channel, the flow transfers itself to other channels, but life goes on. And in this great drama of life renewed, one sees and feels the divine presence, and is at one with it.

Bradford Smith, 1965

In my end is my beginning, and the
way out is the way in.

Damaris Parker-Rhodes, 1985

QUERIES

- *Have I considered how I might love myself even in the midst of the inevitable frailties I will encounter as I die?*

- *Am I prepared for the summons of death—the turning over of my time to eternity?*

- *How do I imagine death: as an ending, a beginning—or both?*

They that love beyond the world
cannot be separated by it.
Death cannot kill what never dies,
nor can Spirits ever be divided
that love and live in the same Divine Principle,
the root and reward of their friendship.

*William Penn, 1693*


I long for household voices gone,
For vanished smiles I long,
But God hath led my dear ones on,
And God can do no wrong.

I know not what the future hath
Of marvel or surprise,
Assured alone that life and death
God's mercy underlies.

*John Greenleaf Whittier, 1865*


The Hassidic Jews have a custom of going out into an open field at night to cry out all their questions and doubts to God, to go down to their basic level of faith. Possibly Jesus was doing this at Gethsemane. Today we may well take the advice of the mother of a dying child who suggested that every hospital should have not only a chapel but a screaming-room. Perhaps this should be the anteroom to the chapel, as in our hearts we have to go through the earthquake and the whirlwind before we are able to hear the still, small voice.

*Carol R. Murphy, 1977*


A God we cannot be honest with is no God. If we bow the head and say, "Thy will be done," when our heart is aflame with protest, we only increase our own pain. Better to rail on God at the passing into the night of this small sweet innocence than to assume unreal acceptance. And then, with small steps, treading the way of sorrows, we may gradually, or perhaps with blinding suddenness, look up from the dark road and see that God has been treading the Way with us, holding us when we faltered, giving us the strength to go hesitatingly forward.

*Sheila Bovell, 1988*

If lovers knew the price of love,
The charge that life to death must pay
Who would not rather turn away?
For heavy days and aching nights
You cost too dear you dear delights.

*Ellen Sophia Bosanquet, 1936*

Grief is the price we pay for love.

*Diana Lampen, 1996*

The secret of finding joy after sorrow—or through sorrow—lies, I think, in the way we meet sorrow itself. We cannot fight against it and overcome it, though often we try and may seem at first successful. We try to be stoical, to suppress our memories . . . to kill [the pain] with strenuous activity so we may be too tired to think. But that is just the time when it returns to us in overwhelming power. . . .

What we must do . . . with God's help is to accept sorrow as a friend, if possible. If not, as a companion with whom we will live for an indeterminate period, for whom we have to make room as one makes room for a guest in one's house, a companion of whom we shall always be aware, from whom we can learn and whose strength will become our strength. Together we can create beauty from ashes and find ourselves in the process.

We do not have to foresee the whole course of the way when we start out with sorrow as our companion. All we have to do is to be genuinely willing to accept God's company for as long as God shall stay with us, to learn from God all that God has to teach us, to live our life quietly and steadily in these new circumstances. We don't do it alone.

*Elizabeth Gray Vining, 1979*

Once, in a time of grief, I learned to love a tree. It began with a line in a poem by Rainer Maria Rilke, written in a time of despair. The poem opens on that note, but then comes this line:

. . . There remains, perhaps,
some tree on a slope
to be looked at
day after day.

I saw hope for myself in that line. Slopes are not easily come by in the flat landscape of Chicago, where we were living, but I found my tree, a maple, and began to look at it, and if I thought no one was looking, I put my arms around it. I felt its rootedness in the earth. I experienced its sensitivity to the slightest breeze. . . . I saw with what celebration it decked itself in bright colors in the fall, and with what grace it let its leaves go, one by one, or in great torrents. It did not lose its integrity, its autonomy, when its leaves were gone, but watched patiently through the winter. I saw the elemental beauty of its bare branches against a leaden sky, and how it embraced the snow. And healing came to me. My tree lived in me and I in it.

*Elizabeth Watson, 1991*


In the years of unemployment I was visiting an educational set-tlement in South Wales, and wished to travel up the valley to another, smaller settlement. The Warden told me to ask Tom, the handyman, who had an old taxi, to take me. Yes, indeed, said Tom, he had the room, but would I be so kind as to sit in the back seat with his wife and hold her hand? On their last holiday together their little only daughter had been drowned, and after weeks of shutting herself away from other people, Tom had at last persuaded his wife to come with him to the upper settlement and give a needed hand with the tea. "You see," said Tom gently, "she doesn't know, as I do, that you can only get over a thing like this by doing what you can for other people." There he stood by his old taxi, my brother in God, with God's love enfolding him and me and his wife, who cried a little in the back seat, but braced herself to pour out tea when we reached the settlement, and was comforted.

*Beatrice Saxon Snell, 1965*

Since you have vanished from my eyes,
Since I have lost your blessed touch,
I own continual surprise
To find, in spite of loss, how much
Of all I cherished still remains:
Your thoughts that set my mind on fire,
And ever flowing in my veins
The urge to do what you require.
Is it that death has more to give
Than love-companioned life can show?
And only as we learn to grieve we learn to know?

*Ellen Sophia Bosanquet, 1948*

The experience of bereavement can take other forms of deprivation. It is not confined to loss of a particular person with whom
one's life was deeply intertwined. Misfortune is versatile and
performs its devastating vivisection on the psyche in other ways
too. . . . Against such vicissitudes one would do well to cultivate
a certain detachment early in life, of the kind Victor Hugo
describes for us:

Be like that bird
Who, pausing in flight,
Feels the bough give way
Beneath her feet
And yet sings,
Knowing she hath wings. . . .

*John Yungblut, 1990*

QUERIES

🔖 *Am I willing to cry out my heart's anguish to God as part of the griev-
ing process?*

🔖 *Do I ask for divine assistance in accepting the unacceptable losses in
my life?*

🔖 *How do I cultivate a spiritual detachment that can help me live into and
through my grief?*

Many times I have found
my way home in the dark
because my feet felt the road
when my eyes could not see it.
There is Something in us,
deeper than hands or feet,
that finds the way to the Central Reality,
and when we arrive we know it.

*Rufus M. Jones, 1944*


I do see the secret work of God
going on in people's minds;
Look not at the hard rocks,
nor look not at briars,
nor look not at the thorns,
nor at the mountains,
nor the coldness,
for well it may be so. . . .
There is a Winter, and there is a Summer;
there is a time to sow the Seed,
there is a time to reap,
so the Lord give thee
an understanding in all things. . . .

*Margaret Fell, 1653*


. . . I know from direct experience that when you are in the last
ditch (mind now, I say *then* and *only* then) you will find art and sci-
ence and the humanities—even human love and help—useless.
You must turn to some final court of appeal and fling your soul on
its mercy. That court of appeal is in yourself, and yet it is *not yourself*, for yourself you are down and out, waiting for the thunderbolt
to fall. This last resort, when your hope is dying and your dignity
dead, will see you through; and when you breathe again and the
horror recedes, you can again find the common consolations

useful to your hand. This is the undoubted truth of the experience which explains such effusions as "O Thou who failest not."

*Damaris Parker-Rhodes, 1977*

It is in my heart to praise thee, O my God;
Let me never forget thee,
what thou has been to me. . . .
When the floods sought to sweep me away
Thou set a compass for them,
how far they should pass over;
When my way was through the sea,
and when I passed under the mountains
there was thou present with me;
When the weight of the hills was upon me
thou upheld me, else had I sunk under the earth;
When I was as one altogether helpless,
when tribulation and anguish was upon me
day and night, and the earth without foundation;
. . . Thou was with me and the Rock of thy Presence.

*James Nayler, 1659*

There is a spirit which I feel that delights to do no evil,
nor to revenge any wrong, but delights to endure
all things, in hope to enjoy its own in the end.
Its hope is to outlive all wrath and contention,
and to weary out all exaltation and cruelty,
or whatever is of a nature contrary to itself.
It sees to the end of all temptations.
As it bears no evil in itself,
so it conceives none in thoughts to any other.
If it be betrayed, it bears it,
for its ground and spring
is the mercies and forgiveness of God.
Its crown is meekness,
its life is everlasting love unfeigned;
it takes its kingdom with entreaty
and not with contention, and

keeps it by lowliness of mind.
In God alone it can rejoice,
though none else regard it, or can own its life.
It's conceived in sorrow,
and brought forth without any to pity it,
nor doth it murmur at grief and oppression.
It never rejoiceth but through sufferings;
for the world's joy it is murdered.
I found it alone, being forsaken.
I have fellowship therein with them
who lived in dens and desolate places in the earth,
who through death obtained
this resurrection and eternal holy life.

*James Nayler, 1660*

Be still and cool
in thy own mind and spirit
from thy own thoughts,
and then thou wilt feel
the principle of God
to turn thy mind to the Lord God,
whereby thou wilt receive God's strength
and power from whence life comes;
whereby thou mayest receive
God's strength to allay
all blusterings, storms, and tempests.

*George Fox, 1658*

Drop Thy still dews of quietness,
Till all our strivings cease;
Take from our souls
the strain and stress,
And let our ordered lives confess
The beauty of Thy peace.

Breathe through the heats
of our desire

Thy coolness and Thy balm;
Let sense be dumb,
let flesh retire;
Speak through the earthquake,
wind and fire,
O still, small voice of calm!

*John Greenleaf Whittier, 1872*


The years ahead will not be peaceful and uneventful.
Those who place too much value on comfort and security
are probably in for a rough time.
Those who are unencumbered and flexible
will more likely survive.

In spite of the "weight of the sad time,"
I bring you a message of hope.
For I believe our young people can yet save the world.
The revolution that is needed now is already taking place
in the minds and lives of some of them.
They have a dream of a somehow strangely better world
than the one they have inherited,
and they are living as if it were already visible, already here.
They step to a different drummer.

*Elizabeth Watson, 1989*


So here is my little nugget of gospel truth for you to take
     home.
The truth is not that it is going to be alright,
the truth is, it already is.

*Fredric Evans, 1994*


QUERIES

& *In the midst of life's tempests and storms, how has hope come to me?*

& *What gives me hope that a brighter future for the world is possible?*

& *In what ways does my life generate hope for others?*

# CHAPTER 5

# Opening Our Hearts

## Through

Longing

Seeking

God

Faith

Prayer

Scripture

A Quaker family living on the American frontier heard a rumor that a Native American war party was planning to attack their small settlement. The other homesteaders barricaded themselves in their houses, loaded their guns, and prepared to do battle. As pacifists, the Quaker family refused to use arms but decided to protect themselves by pulling in the latchstring on their door. When the latchstring was drawn, there was no way for someone from the outside to get in.

When night fell the family went to bed, but found they could not sleep—they were restless, and troubled by doubts. They were worried that by pulling in the latchstring, they were putting their faith in a locked door rather than in God's loving care. Finally they got up, put the latchstring back out the way it usually was, went back to bed, and slept through the rest of the night.

Just before dawn, a war party attacked the settlement. Houses were burned and people were killed, but the homestead with the drawn latchstring was left untouched. The community later heard from Native Americans that the exposed latchstring had been interpreted by the war party as a sign that the Great Spirit was protecting that house—and so, they had left it alone.[12]

Faith in love is difficult, and exposing the latchstring on our hearts is never easy. Many of us have known so little love in life that could be trusted, that it is hard for us to believe in God's promise of covenantal love.

So, we pull in the latchstrings on our hearts, afraid that God's promise of covenantal love does not extend to us. That promise is not that life will always be easy and that we will only walk beside still waters. The promise is that when we walk by faith, we will never walk alone, and that our path will be illumined by an Inward Light. Despite the difficulty, when we open our hearts to plain living, we can trust that our Inner Guide will be there to lead us along the path.

Human yearning for the divine
is as old as we have records,
probably as old as human language.
The yearning suggests we want
to affirm our human bondedness with,
and dependency on, a Divine "Other"
in order to give life meaning
by finding answers to the questions,
Who am I? Where did I come from? . . .
In a prayer of yearning,
it is as if a part of us that
rarely lifts its voice
suddenly finds words and cries out in Truth.

*Candida Palmer, 1983*


Like the deer that pants
for the flowing stream,
so we thirst
for the living Spring.

*Richard J. Foster, 1981*


The whirling dust-wreaths of the street
do not have longings.
The bits of earth crust
which we throw about with our shovel
do not yearn for what is not
and then forthwith construct it.
Desires and strivings,
visions and ideals,
emotions and sentiments,
are as much a genuine part of us
as are the iron and lime
and phosphorus in our bodies. . . .

It is by them that we truly live.
They are revealed through us

rather than created by us.
They find us.
They awaken us.
They break in upon us from beyond us.
They call us forth
to be organs of their revealing.
They enrich us.
They expand us.
They help us to realize our lives
as nothing else does.

*Rufus M. Jones, 1928*


I have felt tender breathings in my soul after God.

*John Woolman, 1744*


A deep-throated bell, muffled or clear, comes ringing in the ears
of our souls from a distant shore in Eternity and awakens in us a
vague uneasiness, a homesickness, a longing. We've all heard that
bell, distant or clear, calling us to a vaster life. Like a wild duck
who has paused to pick at the straws of a barnyard, but who finds
a dim stirring, a homing instinct which makes him leave the sticks
and straws and easy comfortable food for the body and wing his
way into the blue south sky, where lies his home, so do you and I
have a voice within us, a homing instinct of the soul which whis-
pers within us uneasiness and urgency, and the call of Eternity
for our souls. We are all seekers, for we feel that we are sought.

*Thomas R. Kelly, 1940*


QUERIES

- When I listen within to my place of deepest spiritual knowing, what is it
  that I most long for?

- What do my spiritual longings reveal about God's hopes for me?

- Do I understand my spiritual longings as a gift and a nudge from God,
  and do I act on them?

I believe we live in a waiting age
when multitudes are convinced
that something vastly deeper
than they know in the present church
is fundamentally needed.
The land is full of seekers,
the church is full of seekers,
the Society of Friends has its full share of seekers
after genuineness and vitality and integrity
at the base of life which
they have not yet seen illustrated widely.
Such discontent is due not to weakness
but to vision.
Over the horizon they dimly see
something glorious, they know not what.

*Thomas R. Kelly, 1940*

I should like to change the name "seekers" to "explorers." There
is a considerable difference there: we do not "seek" the Atlantic,
we explore it. The whole field of religious experience has to be
explored and has to be described in a language understandable to
modern men and women.

*Ole Olden, 1955*

It is the drama of the Hound of Heaven
baying relentlessly upon our track.
It is the drama of the lost sheep
wandering in the wilderness,
restless and lonely, feebly searching,
while over the hills comes the wiser Shepherd.
For God has a shepherd's heart,
and is restless until all the sheep are safe.
It is the drama of the Eternal God
drawing the prodigal home,

where there is bread enough and to spare.
It is the drama of the Double-Search. . . .
And always its chief actor is—
the Eternal God of Love.

*Thomas R. Kelly, 1939*

The ways to God are many.
They appear when we are ready for them
and when our faithfulness has shown
we can live with the consequences
of further growth.

*John Punshon, 1987*

Give over thine own willing,
give over thine own running,
give over thine own desiring
to know or be anything,
and sink down to the seed
which God sows in thy heart
and let that be in thee,
and grow in thee,
and breathe in thee,
and act in thee,
and thou shalt find by sweet experience
that the Lord knows that
and loves and owns that,
and will lead it to the inheritance of life,
which is God's portion.

*Isaac Penington, 1681*

. . . God is not far away from thee.
Thou, like the inn of old,
hast been full of other guests;
thy affections have entertained other lovers,
wherefore salvation is not yet come to thy house. . . .

*William Penn, 1682*

One thing I understand now is that
one's intellect alone won't pull one through,
and that the greatest service it can perform is
to open a window for that thing
we call the divine spirit.

*Hilda Clark, 1908*

God is always visible
the moment
the inner eye
is clear.

*Rufus M. Jones, 1901*

QUERIES

- *How do I distract myself with busyness in order to avoid the One who is seeking me?*

- *Am I nurturing the seed God has sown in my heart?*

- *Do I live with my eyes and my heart open—watching and listening for the One who seeks me?*

I can remember my own disappointment when it opened out upon me that I was not going to find what I called a proof of God. I wanted something that was irrefutable; some chain of "because" and "therefore" leading up to a triumphant conclusion from which there could be no intellectual escape . . . it seemed simply an evasion to be told that God was most truly to be found in the deepest experiences of life. [But] I have come to see, first, that I shall get no better evidence, and second, that that which I have is good. Intellectual considerations are in no degree whatever to be undervalued and in their place they are invaluable—but, at best, they only point the way, and in themselves they never take us to the end. . . .

*Neave Brayshaw, 1911*

We wanted to do it all. We wanted to control that which gave meaning and power in our lives. In truth, we wanted to provide our own salvation. We wanted a god who would be yet another finite pillar under our control, a god that would take away the terror of facing that empty place which lurked at the limit of all finite things and at the end of our "self." In the dark night that god dies as our narrowly manipulating self dies. More accurately, we recognize that this god has never been there at all, except insofar as we have conjured up such a security blanket. At that moment a new encounter is possible with God who has been waiting in the dark from which we have been fleeing.

*Sandra Cronk, 1991*

I do not accept the idea of the omnipotence of God. If God is all-powerful and did not step in to save people in the gas chambers of Nazi Germany, or children burned by napalm in the jungles of Vietnam, then God has no relevance for me. . . . What do I know about God for sure? That even though God cannot save us from disaster and loss, God suffers with us. This I know experientially. . . .

*Elizabeth Watson, 1991*

The God of our quest is more than a vague Beyond, more than a
bare ultimate Reality. God is a God with concrete character. God
is revealed wherever higher and more ideal forms of life are
conquering and supplanting the lower ones. Wherever the shin-
ing tents of the forces of light are pitched against the armies of
darkness, there God is creating God's new world. God is the God
of beauty and truth. God lives and expresses God's self through
the spirit of love and self-giving. Where love is, God is; and,
therefore, where love is incarnated at its best, there God is most
nearly incarnated. Where the curve of human life rises highest
above the low and mean and cruel, and nearest to the ideal of
unselfish goodness, there God is most clearly to be found. God is
never characterless and abstract. God is infinitely rich in the
concrete.

*Rufus M. Jones, 1928*

Whatever
your mind comes at,
I tell you flat
God is not that!

*Rufus M. Jones, 1947*

God is in the prepositions—
beyond,
among, within,
beneath.

*Sharon Daloz Parks, 1994*

It is we who are known by and in God.
The process of entering
into a deep relationship with God
is also the process of uncovering ourselves.

*Sandra Cronk, 1991*

Christ no longer stands for a Being who came to the world to effect a mysterious scheme of salvation, a scheme to be mediated henceforth by . . . an authoritative church. . . . Christ is God eternally revealing God's self in immediate relationship with us. Christ by his coming did not change the divine attitude; Christ revealed God as God essentially was and is, and made the fact forever plain that God is self-revealing and inwardly present wherever a human life is open and receptive.

*Rufus M. Jones, 1936*

For me, being a Christian means that the life and teaching of Jesus, as recorded in the Gospels, set the standards for our day-to-day living. It points further to the source of the power that sustained Jesus as he followed his way of life. For Quakers to be Christian means that they endeavor to follow—however imperfectly—his sayings. It is not a creed, but a life to be lived in the power of the spirit.

*George A. Selleck, 1978*

Jesus lived a life of love. He taught that love is the motive power of life, and that its application is the solution of all the problems of life. To the challenge of this way of life the spirit within us responds. We accept and make the ideals of Jesus our own. . . . The bond of our religious fellowship is an experience in the soul that God is love.

*Ohio Yearly Meeting, Religious Society of Friends, 1978*

If you were to ask ten Quakers to explain to whom they were listening and speaking in the silence, and just what was their idea of God, I doubt very much whether you would get two identical answers; and I doubt still more whether agnostics would find one answer to satisfy them among the lot. The fact is, that when we try to explain, even to ourselves, what we mean by God, ordinary words fail us.

*Kathleen Lonsdale, 1962*

God is revealed to individuals through models suited to their temperaments and abilities; to communities through models suited to their culture. . . . If there is no one model of the truth and if no model is essential then there is no basis for authoritarianism or heresy-hunts. Our own vision is widened by the vision of others.

Janet Scott, 1980

QUERIES

&  What do I know about God experientially?

&  How does my understanding of God determine the way I live?

&  What images and metaphors for God evoke a sense of Presence and help me focus my spiritual life?

Faith is not seeing light in things that are really dark, against all the evidence; it is understanding the dark as it really is, and taking one's place in the forces that are ranged against it. But we have first, as George Fox found, to discover the ocean of darkness within ourselves, and come through it, with all the spiritual trouble which that entails. There is no easy way.

*John Punshon, 1990*

To embrace a faith that fits us comfortably is a poor way of accepting religion; more than that, it is in a real sense a wrong and pernicious way, for it reverses the true order of things, placing the people who are to be re-formed into the position of the Truth that is to re-form them. It is an impiety that transposes creature and Creator. Faith must be a continuing challenge to which we must respond, a discipline to which we must submit, not a feather bed to protect us against the sharp edge of living.

*Edgar B. Castle, 1961*

When I talk about "practicing our faith," I am thinking about "practice" in the most common use of that term. That is, we have to practice our faith the same way we practice the piano, or practice dancing, or practice a variety of skills and crafts. Our faith is, in many ways, something we learn more about and grow in by doing, by trying to embody or live out our intentions and ideals, and by learning from our failures as well as our successes.

*Thomas Jeavons, 1997*

Lucy E. Harris (1873–1962) became a doctor and went to practice medicine in China. No situation daunted her. . . . Her utter fearlessness in dealing with difficulties sprung from her deep faith in God; not a cozy belief that nothing dangerous would happen to her, but a firm belief that in whatever did happen she would have the presence of God with her. . . .

She once encountered two war-lords with their followers lined up on each side of a river. Lucy, a tiny, slightly-built woman possessing a firm, strong, clear voice, stood in a boat in the middle of the river, shouting to them, insisting that they stop their fighting and go their separate ways. They turned themselves about and went.

*Based on information from Hertford and*
*Hitchin Monthly Meeting, 1961*

I said to one of the Cuban Friends, "It must be hard to be a Christian in Cuba." He smiled. "Not as hard as it is in the United States," he said. Of course, I asked why he said that, and he went on, "You are tempted by three idols that do not tempt us. One is affluence, which we do not have. Another is power, which we also do not have. The third is technology, which again we do not have. Furthermore, when you join a church or a meeting, you gain social acceptance and respectability. When we join, we lose those things, so we must be very clear about what we believe and what the commitment is that we are prepared to make."

*Gordon M. Browne, Jr., 1989*

. . . We don't really want to be dependent on anyone else—even God. We want to be totally self-reliant. One thing I learned in Kenya is that prayer is about humility—about admitting that some things are not in our control. I learned that the opposite of faith is not doubt; rather, the opposite of faith is believing you are always in control. For our Kenyan neighbors, getting money to pay school fees or to buy fertilizer was as much out of their control as whether or not the rains would come, so to pray was a natural response. Because we had resources—a bank account, a vehicle, a phone—things were less often out of our control.

*Tom and Liz Gates, 1995*

Faith is certainly not to be tied up in a tight parcel of "I believes." It is a path along which I have to walk into further truth.

*Damaris Parker-Rhodes, 1985*

Be patterns, be examples in all countries, places, islands, nations, wherever you come; that your carriage and life may preach among all sorts of people and to them; then you will come to walk cheerfully over the world, answering that of God in every one; whereby in them ye may be a blessing, and make the witness of God in them to bless you. . . .

*George Fox, 1656*

. . . There is a living God at the center of all, who is available to each of us, a Present Teacher at the very heart of our lives. We seek as people of God to be worthy vessels to deliver the Lord's transforming word, to be prophets of joy who know from experience and can testify to the world, as George Fox did, "that the Lord God is at work in this thick night." Our priority is to be receptive and responsive to the life-giving Word of God, whether it comes through the written Word—the Scriptures; the Incarnate Word—Jesus Christ; the Corporate Word—as discerned by the gathered meeting; or the Inward Word of God in our hearts which is available to each of us who seek the Truth.

*Epistle of the World Gathering of Young Friends, Greensboro, North Carolina, 1985*

May you learn to understand
the significance of the faith
you profess.

*Marion Sanders, 1994*

Faith . . . is an endless pilgrimage of the heart. We know that our awareness of God's Truth is always beyond our secure apprehension; yet we are committed to seeking after it diligently and then living faithfully according to the measure of Truth given to us.

*Daniel A. Seeger, 1999*

When I took the leap,
I had faith I would find a net;
instead I learned I could fly.

*John Calvi, 1994*


QUERIES

🕊 *Am I willing to work through the "ocean of darkness" within myself in order to deepen my faith?*

🕊 *How do my needs for control and security interfere with my faith journey?*

🕊 *Do I understand my life as a journey of faithfully seeking Truth?*

In prayer it is a matter of being present where we are.

*Douglas Steere, 1962*


To pray is to pay attention to the deepest thing
that we know. . . .
Prayer is a space in which to become truly human.

*Douglas Steere, 1982*


To pray contemplatively is to abandon one's ideas of how and why it all works: God, justice, or prayer. It is to abandon ourselves to trust in the living presence and reality of the divine, mysteriously at work within the darkness of the human condition—a living presence apparently not in the business of straightening out everything as we would do, or to our specifications.

*Patricia Loring, 1997*


We are told that we have only to ask and we shall receive; but we have prayed and prayed and nothing happens. We ask for help to overcome temptation, and then go and do, or say, the very thing we wished to avoid. We wonder what our Lord's promises mean, if they so constantly fail us. Is the grace of God a dream and not a reality?

Then it is that, if we only knew it, God is nearest to us, seeking us with an intensity of which our own longing for God is but a pale reflection. If we cannot at once open our souls to God's love and grace, let us in patience wait for God; and we shall discover at last that it is God who has been infinitely patient with us.

*Edward Grubb, 1933*


My own belief is that outward circumstances are not often (I will not say never) directly altered as a result of prayer. That is to say, God is not always interfering with the working of the natural order. . . . Prayer is not given us to make life easy for us, or to coddle us, but to make us strong. . . . We pray, not to change God's will, but to bring our wills into correspondence with God's.

*William Littleboy, 1937*

A friend tells me that when she prays for someone she does not so much pray *to* God as *for* God for them. This seems to me a vital clue about prayer. It is God that the troubled person needs, not our advice and instructions. As we learn more about worship we learn to listen more deeply so that we can be channels through which God's love reaches the other person.

*Diana Lampen, 1979*

In prayer, the seeds of concern have a way of appearing. Often enough, a concern begins in a feeling of being personally liable, personally responsible, for someone or some event. With it there may come an intimation that one should do some little thing: speak to some person, make an inquiry into a certain situation, write a letter, send some money, send a book. . . . But this seed is given us to follow, and if we do not follow it, we cannot expect to see what may grow from it. Seeds, not fruit, are given in prayer, but they are given for planting.

*Douglas Steere, 1962*

In . . . intercessory prayer there is a consciousness that your act of prayer enters into a great sweep of intercession that is already going on. . . . William Temple, the late Archbishop of Canterbury, speaking of his own practice of intercessory prayer, would say on this point, "When I pray, coincidences happen, and when I do not, they don't." . . .

*Douglas Steere, 1962*

Whose Name I Dare Not Whisper,
may you be known by all peoples.

As You call us forth,
we seek to obey
with the surety of the astral bodies.

Touch us with your gentle love
and forgive us our grief and doubts
at standing alone,
as we forgive your requiring us
to such obedience.

Do not lead us to places
where we will fail You,
but do protect us from all evil.

For your Commonwealth is love,
your power is compassion,
and we thank You.

*Judith L. Brutz, 1990*

Do we pray, or does God pray through us? I know not. All I can say is, prayer is taking place, and we are graciously permitted to be within the orbit.

*Thomas R. Kelly, 1939*

To pray is to be vulnerably open
to God's unpredictable grace.

*Patricia Loring, 1997*

How, then, shall we lay hold of that Life and Power, and live the life of prayer without ceasing? By quiet, persistent practice in turning of all our being, day and night, in prayer and inward worship and surrender, toward the One, who calls in the deeps of our souls. . . . Begin now, as you read these words, as you sit in your chair, to offer your whole selves, utterly and in joyful abandon, in quiet, glad surrender to the One who is within. . . . Walk and talk and work and laugh with your friends. But behind the scenes keep up the life of simple prayer and inward worship. Keep it up throughout the day. Let inward prayer be your last act before you fall asleep and the first act when you awake.

*Thomas R. Kelly, 1941*


By inward sense, by outward signs,
God's presence still the heart divines;
Through deepest joy of God we learn,
In sorest grief to God we turn,
And reason stoops its pride to share
The child-like instinct of a prayer.

*John Greenleaf Whittier, 1871*


QUERIES

- What process do I use to listen and "pay attention to the deepest thing I know"?

- Do I pay attention to the "seeds of concern" for others that may come to me in prayer? Do I act on them?

- Do I look for the "coincidences" that happen when I pray?

The Bible is not the dictator of our conduct and faith. It is rather the record of persons who exemplified faith and virtue. It does for religion that which the dictionary does for speech. Its value consists in its agreement with experience, or with truth, as Friends used to use the word. What is truth in the Bible is there because it is true, not true because it is there. Its experiences "answer" to ours. This is the repeated discovery of generations of Bible readers. "I meet that in Scripture," said Coleridge, "which finds me."

*Henry Cadbury, 1959*

I don't read Scripture to learn doctrine.
I don't read it to find answers to every question.
I read it to find God.

*Carole Spencer, 1999*

"You say Christ saith this, and the apostles say this; but what canst thou say? Art thou a child of light and hast walked in the Light; and what thou speaketh, first inwardly from God," . . .

This opened me so, that it cut me to the heart; and then I saw clearly we were all wrong. So I sat down in my pew again and cried in my spirit to the Lord: "We are all thieves; we are all thieves; we have taken the Scriptures in words, and know nothing of them in ourselves."

*Margaret Fell, 1690*

Within themselves they found the law of right,
They walked by faith and not the letter's sight,
And read their Bibles by the Inward Light.

*John Greenleaf Whittier, 1891*

Friends believe in the Holy Scriptures, but they have never placed them above the Spirit that inspired them. The principle upon which the first Friends placed most emphasis was the Holy Spirit in the hearts of humankind.

*Iowa Yearly Meeting of Friends*
*(Conservative), 1953*

QUERIES

- *What texts and literature are holy for me? Why?*

- *What confers spiritual authority to the texts I consider holy?*

- *Do I read holy texts with the expectation that God will be revealed to me?*

# CHAPTER 6

# Discovering a Spiritual Path

## to Plain Living Through

Contemplative Listening

Everyday Mysticism

Leadings

Discernment

Following a Quaker sense of leading, Stephen Grellet (1773–1855) once traveled many miles through the wilds of western Pennsylvania to pay a pastoral visit to a remote logging camp. After making his solitary journey through the forest, he arrived to find that the loggers had moved on. Stephen did not know what to do and prayed for further guidance. During his prayer, he felt a spiritual nudge to speak, so he stood in the middle of the deserted campsite and delivered a heartfelt and passionate message to the empty clearing.

Years later while traveling in Europe, Stephen was crossing London Bridge when a passing stranger exclaimed, "I know you!" The man explained that many years before, while walking through the Pennsylvania forest, he heard Stephen ministering to an abandoned logging camp and hid in the bushes to listen. Stephen's message went straight to his heart, and his life was forever changed by what he heard.[13]

We never know what we will hear when we listen within; messages from our Inner Guide cannot be anticipated, and they arrive when we least expect them. They may drift in on revealing dreams or come with a gentle nudge; they may also become evident through a growing sense of discomfort or the ending of a relationship, or losing a secure lifestyle, or a job. Sometimes in cases of immediate danger, they are direct and explicit. But most of the time our Inner Guide just issues invitations.

The path to plain living is found by listening for these invitations with "the ears of our heart."[14] These ever-unfolding invitations come as spiritual nudges and stirrings that invite us to be the people our Inner Guide believes we can become.

Silence is the inaudible echo
of the voice of God
which is heard with the ears of the heart.
It is not simply the absence of speech
but a state of being. . . .

*Peter and Carole Fingesten, 1987*

Silence itself, of course, has no magic. It may be just sheer emptiness, absence of words or noise or music. It may be an occasion
for slumber, or it may be a dead form. But it may be an intensi-
fied pause, a vitalized hush, a creative quiet, an actual moment of
mutual and reciprocal correspondence with God. Our actual
meeting with God and God with us is the very crown and culmi-
nation of what we can do with our human life here on earth.

*Rufus M. Jones, 1937*

. . . God is in the here and how. The great saying: "I am that I am"
can also be translated: "I will be present where I will be present."
And, if we are to be ready for this presence, we must be able
to . . . listen. How else can we hear God, if we are not capable of
inner silence?

*Carol R. Murphy, 1974*

*For Listening Within*

. . . [We] may use a variety of methods, using whichever one[s]
seem appropriate at any given time. Yet, in spite of all this seem-
ing variety and lack of a single practice, most of these approach-
es include three important qualities:

~  The first is *desire*, a profound yearning to be in the
   Presence. . . .

~  The second is *focus*. Whatever technique or lack of technique
   people may use during these opening moments of worship,

they all aim toward a relaxed, alert attentiveness in the presence of God.

~ And the third is *trust*, a synonym of faith, for it takes trust to go out into the deep water; it takes trust to let go and rest or float in the Deep and Living Water of the Stream.

*William Taber, 1992*


To pray contemplatively is to give ourselves over to trust that it is sufficient for us to labor to be open and responsive to the level at which this divinity is present and working within and through us and all things. It is to accept a place in a living process whose end or shape is beyond our comprehension.

*Patricia Loring, 1997*


Silence is simply a preparation for being still. . . . We are able to discern the Spirit because of the stillness of our hearts, not because our bodies are motionless.

*Based on John Punshon, 1987*


The mind wanders and the will falters again and again. Even the great masters of the religious life have confessed they were always liable to be invaded by the most frivolous thoughts during their meditations. . . . A mother does not condemn her child who is struggling with many a failure to learn how to walk, but rather she is pleased by each successful effort.

*Thomas F. Green, 1952*


Contemplation may lead eventually to bliss, but first it will give us the pain of knowing that some of our dearest convictions are shallow, inadequate, wrong. Contemplation first deprives us of familiar comforts. Then it replaces them with an inner emptiness in which new truth, often alien and unsettling truth, can emerge. The contemplative journey from illusion to reality may have peace as its destination, but en route it usually passes through some fearsome places.

*Parker J. Palmer, 1990*

Silence creates its own tensions,
it fluctuates like waves;
after every high there is a low,
even soft murmurs as its
waves dissipate toward the shore.
You may step into the pool of silence
denuded and in pain but you will emerge from it
restored in truth and peace.

*Peter and Carole Fingesten, 1987*

It is idle to ask those who never listen
whether and how God answers prayer.

*Caroline Stephen, 1891*

The way to hear the language of the Spirit
is to be within;
it is often slow of utterance
unless we are willing and obedient;
the quicker we are to hear
and active in obeying,
the readier and oftener
it speaks to our instruction. . . .

*Samuel Neale, 1771*

QUERIES

- Do I cultivate the qualities of desire, focus, and trust in my practice of contemplative listening?

- Am I willing to face my inner emptiness in contemplation so that new truth may emerge?

- Am I willing to obey the still, small voice within when it speaks to my instruction?

God doesn't usually tell us what to do in so many words. But it's amazing how the world offers nudges once we ask! Suddenly, books open to significant passages. Being with our child brings an awareness. Chance events reveal opportunities to give our gifts or satisfy our needs. Messages may come during dreams, meditation, or prayer, in the form of images, words, or feelings in our bodies. Or we may wake up one morning with that feeling of knowing. We find God by paying attention to the present moment.

*Julie Shaul, 1999*

When I first arrived in my new home, I sensed I was being asked not to take a job yet but to spend time in inner work. As my savings became depleted, I became fearful and complained to God. In a dream a patient voice asked if I could wait a little while longer. In a subsequent dream I was looking for a student at the Community College of Philadelphia. I had never heard of such a place and was surprised when I later heard a subway conductor announce a stop as the location of that very college. Then one morning I woke with an image of the Sunday paper in my mind and the certainty that I should apply for a job listed in the classifieds that day. Only one job in that paper matched my qualifications: a position teaching at the Community College of Philadelphia. I was hired and taught there for years.

*Marcelle Martin, 1996*

Once at sea, in the middle of the night, when all unbeknown to me then my little boy, left behind in America, was dying, with no father by him to hold his hand, I suddenly felt myself surrounded by a mighty presence and held as though by invisible arms. At no other time in my life have I ever felt such positive contact, and on this occasion my entire being was calmed, and I was inwardly prepared to meet the message of sorrow which waited for me next day when I landed at Liverpool. It may be said, no doubt, that this and all such experiences are only intuitive flashes from one's own submerged deposits of memory, imagination, and emotion. I can only answer, yes, it may be so; but it may also be true as well that in such moments, when the inner self is unified and heightened in its powers of apprehension, some real influx of life and energy from beyond the margins of our own being may break in and find us.

*Rufus M. Jones, 1928*

I had my first mystical experience when I was in labor with my son. At some point during the delivery, I moved into a higher state of consciousness. I had an image of riding ocean waves into the shore, and I felt lifted beyond the pain which helped me rise above the difficulty of the contractions. I had an awake and almost pain-free delivery. I needed no anesthesia—nothing. I was very awake and in that heightened sense of Presence, I knew for the first time that God was in me, and that this was God's child as much as it was mine.

*Based on conversation with Mary Hillas, 2000*

To some the truth of God never comes
closer than a logical conclusion. . . .
To the mystic God becomes real
in the same sense that
experienced beauty is real,
or the feel of spring is real,
or that summer sunlight is real. . . .

*Rufus M. Jones, 1922*

My uncle George Warner, who was born in the nineteenth century, was both well educated and widely traveled. One day during meeting for worship in Germantown, Pennsylvania, Uncle George rose to speak and surprised his family and the meeting by speaking his message in French.

When the service ended, a stranger rose from the back of the room and said in French, "I read, but do not speak English. This morning when I walked by your sign and read 'The Society of Friends,' I thought to myself, maybe someone in there will be a friend to me. I was desperate and felt ready to end my life. I entered the meeting house and was sitting quietly in prayer, when suddenly someone rose and spoke in French the words of comfort I most needed to hear."

*Barbara Cummings St. John, 1997*

It now seems that the mystic's experience of timelessness, self-loss, and union with the whole is shared by more people than one might expect, regardless of their religious upbringing. Many assert that we all have mystical potentiality, that we all can at least have what Abraham Maslow called "peak experiences," . . . the "mystical" way of knowing is field-knowing, in which relation-ship[s] . . . are seen to be primary, and we are all members of one another. Telepathy and spiritual healing become possible, not as mysterious "powers" but as direct perception and actualization of interconnectedness.

*Carol R. Murphy, 1977*

Mystics . . . are not peculiarly favored mortals who by a lucky chance have received into their lives a windfall from some heavenly Breadfruit tree, while they lay dreaming of iridescent rainbows. They are, rather, people who have cultivated, with more strenuous care and discipline than others have done, the native homing passion of the soul for the Beyond. . . .

*Rufus M. Jones, 1928*

QUERIES

❧ *Do I attempt to stay mindfully and spiritually present to each moment?*

❧ *Do I listen to the insights that come to me from beyond the margins of my understanding? How do I know when to act on them?*

❧ *Am I cultivating a discipline of listening and watching so that I recognize the messages that come to me through dreams, prayers, meditations, friends, or my own body?*

Leading and being led: the words are simple enough. . . . They say that it is not only possible but essential to our nature for human beings to hear and obey the voice of God; that we can be direct-ed, daily, in what we do, the jobs we hold, the very words we say; and that our obedience may draw us to become leaders in all spheres of human life—in the professions, arts and sciences, but also in discovering the ethical, political, and social and economic consequences of following the will of God.

*Paul A. Lacey, 1985*

We must learn to put our trust in God and the leadings of the Spirit. How many of us are truly led by the Spirit throughout our daily lives? I have turned to God when I have had a difficult deci-sion to make or when I have sought strength to endure the pain in dark times. But I am only slowly learning to dwell in the place where leadings come from. That is a place of love and joy and peace, even in the midst of pain. The more I dwell in that place, the easier it is to smile, because I am no longer afraid.

If we dwell in the presence of God, we shall be led by the spir-it. We do well to remember that being led by the spirit depends not so much upon God, who is always there to lead us, as upon our willingness to be led.

*Gordon Matthews, 1987*

A leading does not come to us simply so we may have one. Eventually its inwardness takes outward form and affects the rest of the human community. When we are led to truth it is so we may live *by* it and do something *with* it.

*Paul A. Lacey, 1985*

I was driving home one day when I suddenly felt a nudge to stop at a florist shop and buy a large bouquet of flowers in honor of my father. Although he had died many years before, this was his birthday and I was feeling very close to him.

On my way home with the flowers, I saw a woman striding along beside the road. There was nothing extraordinary about her, and I would normally not even have noticed her, but something about the tense way she was walking led me to pull over and ask her if she needed help. When I asked her if there was anything I could do for her, she told me that her sister had just died. She said the two of them had lived together for years, and she was beside herself with grief. I drove her back to her house, and before I left, I gave her my bouquet of flowers. It seems to me that miracles are all in the timing.

*Barbara Cummings St. John, 2000*

Proceed as Way opens.

*Quaker Saying*

### How to Recognize a Leading

When God taps me on the shoulder . . . when something in our lives grabs me and won't let go.

Leadings start from where we are, from something which touches our lives and hearts in some way, not from an abstract notion.

We cannot rest easy without responding, or feeling pain or guilt in the denial of action.

Leadings rarely include instruction sheets or directions. The specifics only develop as the way opens.

A true leading also involves patience and a willingness to be tested and to be accountable to our meeting community.

The witness to the Light Within gives us the courage to be faithful, no matter what the consequences.

Remembering not to run ahead of our Inward Teacher is difficult, but it is also essential to faithful action. The results of our actions are not ours to control.

*Based on information*
*from Margery Post Abbot, 1995*

Being guided isn't like making a cake, where you mix it up and sit back until it's baked. It's more like dancing with a partner. If you're not following continual subtle motions, you aren't being led. . . .

*Julie Shaul, 1999*

## Hallmarks of a Leading

1. First of all, the leading is directed inwardly. The tight control we may have kept on our inner doubts becomes loosened, and confusion threatens to overwhelm us. . . . Through all this turmoil we become aware of a great longing to know what can be depended on, and we recognize that our desire to know what is true is greater even than our desire to be comforted.

2. A second hallmark of a leading is that we recognize that our endurance comes as a gift, an opening. The waiting is still painful, but our capacity to resist false answers gives us some assurance a true one will come.

3. A third hallmark is that we learn about people. As we come to know our own condition, we come also to know the condition of others. . . . To know our own condition and the conditions of others is to have a realistic view of human frailties and also to know the witness within each of us which can lead us out of error.

4. A fourth hallmark of a leading is that we feel ourselves increasingly under obedience. A gathering power of conviction within us sustains our courage and patience and then points us to first steps in a re-ordering of our lives. And as we persevere in obedience, we may find that the steps we feel drawn to take become bigger, more defined. We feel more clearly led.

*Paul A. Lacey, 1985*

Throughout Quaker journals we find frequent reference to the absence of inward peace as a sign that some "concern" [leading], possibly to undertake a journey [or] engage in some effort for social reform, had been laid upon the individual. . . . It is not essential that the undertaking be successful for inward peace to result. It is only necessary that the individual feel that he or she has done all that they are able to do to carry out the requirement. . . . God only demands that we live up to our capacity.

*Howard Brinton, 1948*


His [John Woolman's] visit to the Indians begins with "inward drawings" to them in the fall of 1761. In the winter of 1762 he first shares his feelings with his several meetings and "having the unity of Friends," he begins arrangements in the spring of 1763 to travel that summer. . . . While on the journey, he reflects on the dangers facing him—death or captivity by the Indians—and examines both his fears and motives rigorously. . . .

Woolman is mature and seasoned in the truth, but even so he is not selfless by nature. He becomes so by probing and acknowledging every tincture of self-will and then offering it up to God.

This perfectly summarizes the characteristics of a true leading. It begins inwardly, as a process or motion of caring whose direction and object are unclear, so a time of waiting must occur, during which Woolman rigorously examines himself, learns his limitations and frailties but also his strengths, and achieves patience and perseverance. From that patient waiting a concern arises and becomes clarified and directed until it leads to an action on behalf of others.

*Paul A. Lacey, 1985*


In retrospect I realize that my leading to build a co-housing project had been growing in me since I was a child. Even though I had this lifelong leading to offer my skills as a developer in service to the community to build co-housing, I was hesitant and anxious about it because I knew the task would be a complicated undertaking. I felt a pit in the bottom of my stomach, and it felt like jumping off a high diving board when I finally met with the Clerk of Cambridge Meeting. But she was supportive and suggested that I write to Ministry and Counsel to request a clearness committee to help me discern my leading.

The meeting's recognition and support of my leading helped me stay clear and feel like it was okay to keep moving ahead as way opened. Ultimately the project did come together, and all during construction I continued to seek clearness and felt connected to the Meeting on many different levels, right up to the completion and opening of our co-housing complex in 1998.

As I look back on the whole process now I realize that it is easier to stick your neck out and be brave, knowing mistakes are inevitable, when you have a sense of leading. Creating a co-housing community included the challenges of locating a good site, securing financing, and developing a process for co-housing members to make decisions as a group. All along I knew that I was creating more than a form of co-housing; it was a way of living that imbued certain values I associated with my Quaker beliefs, especially with respect to environmentally sustainable urban living. My experience in faithfully following my leading with the support and discernment of the Meeting further convinced me that the way we live in community shapes the way we relate to the rest of the world.

*Based on conversation with Gwendolen Noyes, 2000*

We need to be willing to be led into the dark as well as through green pastures and by still waters. We do not need to be afraid of the dark, because God is there. The future of this earth need not be in the hands of the world's "leaders." The world is in God's hands if we are led by God. Let us be led by the Spirit.

*Gordon Matthews, 1987*

In 1938, Rufus Jones, George Walton, and Robert Yarnall followed a shared leading to Germany to meet with the German SS about releasing Jews. Because Friends had initiated a massive feeding program in Germany after World War I, they had reason to hope the Germans would believe in their good will.

The three men said they had come "to inquire in the most friendly manner whether there is anything we can do to promote life . . . and to relieve suffering.". . . After hearing their requests, the SS officers left the room to confer. The three Americans

bowed their heads "and entered upon a time of deep, quiet meditation and prayer" while they waited for the officers to return.
Later they learned that their room had been bugged and their
"silence" had confirmed the earnestness of their mission.

They were then told that they could proceed with their work
of Jewish evacuation and that other Quaker representatives
would be permitted to travel unhindered throughout Germany
and Austria to implement their purpose. In the U.S., the entire
mission was seen as a breakthrough. . . . The Quakers received a
grant to finance the work of a new team of Quakers to be sent to
Germany, and plans were drafted for a camp to house refugees
receiving visas to the U.S. But the plans were never realized
because American politicians decided not to accept the refugees.

*Based on information from Hans A. Schmitt,*
*1997*

Charity Cook (1745–1822) had a sister, Susannah Hollingsworth,
who was about to leave on a trip to England. As the two sisters
sat on shipboard for a few minutes in prayer and meditation,
Charity suddenly told her sister that she should not take passage
on that ship. Susannah respected Charity's warning and left the
ship with her luggage to wait for another ship. The vessel on
which Susannah had first booked passage sailed and was never
heard from again.

*Based on information from Carol and*
*John Stoneburner, 1986*

A concern [leading] is God-initiated, often surprising, always
holy, for the life of God is breaking through into the world. Its
execution is in peace and power and astounding faith and joy, for
in unhurried serenity the Eternal is at work in the midst of time,
triumphantly bringing all things unto God's self.

*Thomas R. Kelly, 1941*

QUERIES

℞ *How open am I to being led by the Spirit in my daily life?*

℞ *Before following a leading, am I willing to prayerfully probe my motives and acknowledge my self-will? Do I ask for divine assistance in turning over my self-will?*

℞ *Am I faithful in following my leadings? Am I supportive of the leadings of others?*

Discernment is that fallible, intuitive gift we use in attempting to discriminate the course to which we are personally led by God in a given situation, from our other impulses and from the generalized judgments of conscience. Discernment is a gift from God, not a personal achievement. In a life lived with other priorities, the gift may be left underdeveloped. But as we grow and are faithful in the spiritual life we may well be given more.

*Patricia Loring, 1992*

Spiritual discernment is
the process of sifting divine guidance
from other influences:
from internal forces such as fear or selfishness
to external pressures and expectations.
A willingness to listen and
to let go of our own agendas
can help us sift through
all the voices we hear and
discern how God is leading us.

*Eileen Flanagan, 1999*

We meet as we do because we believe that gathered together we are capable of greater clarity of vision. It is therefore the practice in our society for a Friend who, after due consideration, believes that he or she has a concern [leading], to bring it before the gathered community of Friends. This is both a further part of the testing process and an expression of our membership in a spiritual community. It is a recognition of mutual obligations: that of a Friend to test the concern against the counsel of the group and that of the group to exercise its judgment and to seek the guidance of God.

*Britain Yearly Meeting, 1995*

Quakerism is peculiar in being a group mysticism,
grounded in Christian concepts.

*Howard Brinton, 1952*


Sane mystics do not exalt their own experiences over historical
revelation, they rather interpret their own openings in the light of
the master-revelations.

*Rufus M. Jones, 1909*


You get fired up with a leading, and you have to test it against
your faith community. Sometimes it's just like cold water. And
then you have to go back and fire it up again. But that process
makes you stronger and more flexible.

As the image of tempering was growing in me, I remembered
being touched in a very deep place when I heard these words spoken in a meeting for worship: "We can feel ourselves walking
through fire without being consumed. All that is unnecessary is
burned away and we are left with the strength of a tempered
heart." Now that is a kind of strength that can transform the
world!

*Janet Hoffman, 1990*


The first obligation of the person who has had a leading to the
truth is to test it; the second is to testify to it. Test and testimony are an ongoing, recursive process, continually refreshed in
worship.

*Paul A. Lacey, 1985*


I was offered the opportunity to become the president of a small
educational institution. So as is the custom in the Quaker community, I called on half a dozen trusted friends to help me discern my vocation by means of a "clearness committee," a process
in which the group refrains from giving you advice but spends
three hours asking you honest, open questions to help you discover your own inner truth.

Halfway into the process, someone asked, "What would you like most about being a president?" The simplicity of that question loosed me from my head and lowered me into my heart. "Well, I would not like having to give up my writing and my teaching. . . . I would not like the politics of the presidency. . . . I would not like. . . ." Gently but firmly, the person who had posed the question interrupted me: "May I remind you that I asked what you would most like?" I resumed my sullen but honest litany, "I would not like having to give up my summer vacations. . . . I would not like. . . ." Once again the questioner called me back to the original question. But this time I felt compelled to give the only honest answer I possessed. "Well," said I, in the smallest voice I possess, "I guess what I'd like most is getting my picture in the paper with the word president under it."

I was sitting with seasoned Quakers who knew that though my answer was laughable, my mortal soul was clearly at stake! They did not laugh at all but went into a long and serious silence—a silence in which I could only sweat and inwardly groan. Finally my questioner broke the silence with a question that cracked all of us up—and cracked me open: "Parker," he said, "can you think of an easier way to get your picture in the paper?" I called the school and withdrew my name.

*Based on information from Parker J. Palmer, 2000*

Several years ago I experienced a leading that began with a nudge to help middle-class Americans whose primary meaning and motivation in life is to be consumers. I felt a great tenderness toward these people and began to wonder how I might help them redefine their goals and understand that they already have enough. I wondered if I could help them see that what they were really seeking was a sense of spiritual fulfillment.

I was afraid to follow this leading at first. I didn't think that I was good enough for God to use me in this work. However, the sense of being led would not go away and I finally found the courage to ask my Meeting for a clearness committee to test my leading. Discerning and praying with the committee energized me spiritually and strengthened me in my work. I now lead workshops and teach people an alternative version of financial intelligence with the purpose of helping them make meaning in their lives.

I am deeply grateful for those who have discerned with me over the last seven years. I continue to try to be faithful in my personal, ongoing discernment by taking quiet time most mornings to do spiritual reading, journaling, and to reflect on the previous day by responding to the following queries:

Where in this day did I feel the presence of God working in my life and in the world?

What in this day seemed like it was a part of my leading?

What made me believe that?

How does that leading fit into my personal and spiritual life?

What did I do today to feed my spirit or move me ahead on my spiritual journey?

*Based on conversation with*
*Penny Yunuba, 2000*

### Tests for Discerning the Strength (or Validity) of a Leading

~ The test of *moral purity*. This is the test which would most stringently examine whether too much self-interest, or not enough moral consistency, tainted either an individual's or a group's leading.

~ The test of *patient waiting*. Self-will is impatient of tests.

~ The test of the *self-consistency of the spirit*, which is applied by testing an individual's or meeting's leadings against scriptural analogues and the witness of other Friends. The belief underlying this test is that, though revelation is progressive, God does not change over time.

~ The test of *bringing the group (or individual) into unity*. This test assumes that a true leading will bring with it what St. Paul, writing to the Galatians, calls the fruits of the Spirit: "love, joy, peace, patience, kindness, goodness, faithfulness, gentleness, self-control" (Galatians 5:22-23).

*Hugh Barbour, 1964*

QUERIES

- *What process and criteria do I use to determine whether a feeling or idea is coming from God or from my own personal needs?*

- *Am I willing to test my leading by tempering it in a discernment process with others?*

- *Are the tests of moral purity, patient waiting, self-consistency of the spirit, and group unity part of my discernment process?*

# CHAPTER 7

Growing Together in

Community

Decision-Making

Struggle and Conflict Resolution

Reconciliation and Forgiveness

The Quaker community in Cambridge had gathered to say farewell to Tim and Mary Ann Nicholson, beloved members who were moving to a retirement community in another state. As the farewell reception got underway, a college professor in a dark suit chatted about the Gulf War with a peace activist in bicycle shorts, a ninety-year-old artist discussed her latest show with a mother feeding her new baby, and a tax attorney listened attentively to a homeless man who sometimes dropped by the meeting house looking for food and seeking friendship.

When the program began, those assembled were invited to share remembrances about Tim and Mary Ann. Tim seemed embarrassed, even slightly bewildered, as if he did not quite understand what all the fuss was about. When it was time for him to respond, he gazed around the room in his steady way and in a clear and humble voice said, "Friends, I don't know what to say. It is I who should be thanking you, for without you, how would I have grown?" Tim's words reminded the community how much they had helped one another mature in the presence of the One who had initiated the invitation to grow together.

After Tim's response a hush came over the room as those gathered reflected silently and gratefully on the times of welcoming one another's babies, crying at memorial services, struggling with one another through difficult decisions in business meetings, forgiving each other's shortcomings, and standing side by side in controversial peace vigils.

Living as a community brings deep joy, and personal and corporate growth, but it requires patience, forbearance, speaking truth in love, engaging in conflict, and seeking reconciliation and forgiveness. It involves learning to deal with tensions and conflict and building a communal Center from which we can witness and support one another on our individual and corporate paths to plain living.

Ideally, our Friends meetings are covenant communities. It is God who gives us to one another and to the community. Our relationship with others is divinely mediated.

*Annis Bleeke, 1999*

In true community we will not choose our companions, for our choices are so often limited by self-serving motives. Instead, our companions will be given to us by grace. Often they will be persons who will upset our settled view of self and world. In fact, we might define true community as that place where the person you least want to live with lives! . . .

Community reminds us that we are called to love, for community is a product of love in action and not of simple self-interest. Community can break our egos open to the experience of a God who cannot be contained by our conceptions. Community will teach us that our grip on truth is fragile and incomplete, that we need many ears to hear the fullness of God's word for our lives. And the disappointments of community life can be transformed by our discovery that the only dependable power for life lies beyond all human structures and relationships.

In this religious grounding lies the only real hedge against the risk of disappointment in seeking community. That risk can be borne only if it is not community one seeks, but truth, light, God. Do not commit yourself to community, but commit yourself to God. . . . In that commitment you will find yourself drawn into community.

*Parker J. Palmer, 1977*

Mind that which is eternal,
which gathers your hearts
together up to the Lord,
and lets you see that
ye are written in one another's heart.

*George Fox, 1652*

Community is a place where the connections felt in the heart make themselves known in bonds between people, and where the tugging and pulling of those bonds keep opening up our hearts.

*Parker J. Palmer, 1977*


Faith community:
creating a space
where obedience to truth
can be practiced.

*Sharon Daloz Parks, 1994, adapted from Parker Palmer*


We admit that our community life has included pettiness, insensitivity, harsh judgments, and irresponsibility. We have spoken when we might better have been silent, and we have been silent when we might better have spoken. We left things to God when we could have helped, and we have tried to do it all ourselves when we could have turned to God. We acknowledge that at times even our weaknesses have been used to God's purposes.

*Beth Bussiere-Nichols, Portland Friends Meeting State of Society Report for 1999*


In community we soon come up against all kinds of experiences that challenge our own ego-definitions. People do not concur with our notions of what is right and good. . . . These problems are made more intractable because we respond to them out of fear, anger, frustration, and all the wounded places in our own lives. We soon discover that there is no way to build our image of the loving, faithful community out of our own strength. We are brought humbly to a sense of emptiness, darkness, absence, and loss. Paradoxically, it is often then that we turn, in our weakness and repeated failure, to God. . . . Only then does it become possible for us to accept God's gift of life in community.

*Sandra Cronk, 1991*

A culture of isolated individualism produces mass conformity because people who think they must bear life all alone are too fearful to take the risks of self-hood. But people who know that they are embedded in an eternal community are both freed and empowered to become who they were born to be.

*Parker J. Palmer, 1990*


We know, with varying degrees of acceptance into awareness, our own weaknesses, and there is a tendency to think that others— who seem, on the surface, to be very sure and confident—do not struggle in the way we do. But many of those who appear to cope and be strong and tireless are indeed very different behind their masks. We are all wounded; we all feel inadequate and ashamed; we all struggle. But this is part of the human condition; it draws us together, helps us to find our connectedness.

*June Ellis, 1986*


Safety in a community gets defined by how the most marginal person in the community is treated. We all believe that if people could see into our hearts and know who we really are, we too might be rejected, so we notice how those at the margins are welcomed.

*Emily Sander, 1992*


Our life is love, and peace, and tenderness;
and bearing one with another,
and forgiving one another,
and not laying accusations
one against another;
but praying one for another,
and helping one another
up with a tender hand. . . .

*Isaac Penington, 1667*

*Advices About Living in Community*

~ When there is difficulty, look first for the good in people's motivations.

~ Just listening to someone can be healing for them.

~ Do not look to human relationships for justice; there are few entities more unjust.*

~ Some people can't understand why their actions hurt others; explanations confuse them, but saying what it is they shouldn't do can be helpful.

~ We all learn best when we are loved, so we should avoid disciplining someone we are not able to love.

~ When people are unkind to you, listen for the portion of truth your friends might not articulate.

~ Love without truth is chaos, but truth without love is cruelty.*

~ Find a good friend (Friend) who will listen to you with love.

~ Look for the humor and watch for the miracles.*

~ Be aware of the pervasive presence of the Spirit, the beauty and struggle in life, and the Mystery which soon engulfs the few things we think we've learned.*

*Emily Sander, 1993[15]*

All of us . . . are diminished and dishonored when we do not meet each other half way. How can we love in truth and lovingly help one another in this? Because we must remember that truth without love is violence. And love without truth is sentimentality. We do need both.

*Muriel Bishop, 1990*

Meeting became a school for faithfulness,
a way of directing my attention
away from myself towards God,
so it would be possible to look for

the person God wanted me to be,
and into which I had to grow. . . .
I came to understand why
it is impossible to be a Quaker without a meeting.

*John Punshon, 1987*

We have a long, long way to go.
So let us hasten along the road,
the roads of human tenderness and generosity.
Groping, we may find
one another's hands in the dark.

*Emily Greene Balch, 1955*

QUERIES

- When there are difficulties in the community, do I hold the community in prayer and remember to look for the good in people's motivations?

- How well do I reach out to the people who are difficult and who live on the margins of my community? What can I learn from them?

- How does my community support me in becoming the person God hopes I will become? How well do I support others?

In meetings for conducting the business of the Society [of Friends] a decision can be made only when those present reach a state of unity. No vote is taken. A vote might represent the coercion of a minority by a majority. It may take weeks or even years to attain such unity. If a group has achieved a truly nonviolent frame of mind, unity is eventually possible because every member has access to the same Light of Truth. This Light is not divided, it is One. This peculiar method, while slower than the process of voting, is more creative, for it gives time for a new point of view to arise out of the syntheses of old ones. It is more durable for the very reason that it represents a greater degree of convincement on the part of the group as a whole.

*Howard Brinton, 1966*


The basis of discernment in a meeting for business is unity. The unity sought is not simple agreement, consensus, compromise, or irreducible minimum of views. What is sought is a sense of that deep, interior unity which is a sign the members are consciously gathered together in God and may therefore trust their corporate guidance. The experience known as the gathered meeting for worship is the basis of unity in the context of the meeting for worship for the conduct of business. Friends have traditionally so valued the fruit of group discernment [sense of the meeting] that they have been willing to labor hard and to wait long to come into unity with one another before proceeding in a matter of substance.

*Patricia Loring, 1992*


In our . . . meetings for worship with attention to business, and meetings for worship in committee, we are seeking Truth: the truth present in the gathered community of faith. Our primary purpose is not to "make decisions," but to affirm the truth of our particular community of faith in a way which builds up that community.

*Janet Hoffman, 1989*

"Open my eyes that I may see
Visions of truth thou has for me.
Open my heart, illumine me, spirit divine."

I think our hope is that into our business meetings, those very temporal happenings, we can bring some "vision of truth." Such a hope must be founded on a sense that sacredness is everywhere, that we are standing on holy ground, and that our task is to perceive it—to take off our shoes, as Moses instructed, and stand in the midst of holiness. We are, in this work, through our workaday lives and the business of the Meeting, to bring time and the timeless together. In even the smallest thing we can be channels for divine love—"not even a sparrow falls, but thou are mindful of it." We must pray,

"Open my heart, illumine me. . . ."

*Ellie Foster, 1986*

Now we are human, and we do come to Business Meeting with our minds made up and our egos strident. I don't think we even need to be terribly distressed when our first statements are from that place of egocentricity; at least that gives us the value of many unique perspectives. But that first expression of human selfness must then be let go. The Meeting must be freed to do its work. Humility is essential before we can melt into and lose ourselves in the search for truth. . . .

*Ellie Foster, 1986*

In our meetings for business, I find people seem to fear that the integrity of their own insight is threatened if the group insight is different. For me, when an individual in a meeting for business reveals the measure of light given to them and the measure of light given to the group as a whole is different, each has its own integrity. The sense of the meeting can be different from that of the individual, and the integrity of the individual's leading is not impugned. The individual who differs may speak in a prophetic voice, like John Woolman, or such persons may be speaking out of human fear or cultural conditioning.

*Janet Hoffman, 1991*

A particularly heavy responsibility falls upon the individual
Friend who disagrees with the sense of the meeting. He or she
must decide whether to dissent silently, to express personal reservations, or to protest the decision strongly and decline to with-
draw one's reservations. Anyone who has taken the last course is
likely to remember it for a long time. And when these occasions
arise, the whole meeting is called upon to ponder not only the
Friendly "weight" of the dissenter, but also the subtle difference
between unanimity and unity.

*Merille Mcaffee Towl, 1977*

Friends often find themselves most challenged when matters
before them call forth strongly held but incompatible responses.
A Meeting which goes forward for whatever reason without real
unity in the Spirit does so at its peril. When any member present
feels so strongly led as to wish to prevent the Meeting from act-
ing, it is important that the Meeting take the time to test this leading in a loving spirit, and examine responsibly the consequences
if the action is not taken.

*Philadelphia Yearly Meeting of the Religious
Society of Friends, 1998*

It is not in differing from one another
that disunity arises—
it is in not listening to God
and each other.

*Kenneth Sutton, 1989*

One reason that Friends' conduct of business is so slow is that it
takes time to sift ourselves and the matter at hand for ego, self-
will, sincere mistakes, matters of individual conscience, and for
reasons which may be excellent intellectually but not necessarily
God's will. In a meeting which is seeking at the deepest level,
there must be time and opportunity for all these matters to rise
to the surface, to be examined in the Light, and to settle again to
a deeper level of quiet. . . . There must be time for change to take
place inwardly—not just in the head but in the heart and gut—as

members search the matter and are searched by it. For no one can come with sincerity to a Friends' gathering for business with a mind unalterably set. To do so would leave no room for the Spirit to move, for Way to open, for discernment to take place.

*Patricia Loring, 1993*

QUERIES

🖎 When I come to meetings with a strong opinion about an issue, do I ask for divine assistance in listening for new insights that God might reveal through the insights of others?

🖎 Do I remember that the primary purpose of group discernment is not to "make decisions" but to discover and affirm the truth for the community?

🖎 Do I have sufficient trust in group discernment that I can accept the group's decision with equanimity and peace?

The commitment to mutual discipline as well as encouragement is based on the recognition that the Light is often more clearly discerned by many than by one. Thus keeping each other in the Light may require constructive, mutual criticism as well as self-criticism. . . . Acceptance of criticism and admission of the need for support require trust and a willingness to be vulnerable, which points back to the importance of basing a friendly notion of discipline on speaking truth in love.

*Thomas H. Jeavons, 1981*

Historically it was through the mutual support
and care of members that
Friends were enabled to stand against
the value systems of the larger society.
The process of mutual accountability
was not a way of checking to see
whether Friends lived up to
certain petty points of lifestyle,
but a way to give each other the strength
to be a people who listened to God and
lived God's new order.

*Sandra Cronk, 1991*

. . . [When] we stop judging the other by our own rules of the game, we [can] accept the fact that there are different games being played according to different rules. Without adopting the other's code, we no longer question their honesty when they follow it honestly; indeed, we respect them for it. We begin to grasp that many concepts on the other side are not due to hypocrisy, ill-will, and hostility, but to the existence of a different code.

*Richard K. Ullmann, 1963*

It must be remembered that bitter criticism
is more hurtful to those who indulge in it

than to those of whom it is uttered . . .
also that remarks uttered half in jest
may have more effect than is imagined
on the younger members of the circle.
Seek ever to speak truth in love.

*London Yearly Meeting, 1925*

Search thine own heart: what paineth thee
In others, in thyself may be;
All dust is frail, all flesh is weak;
Be thou the true person thou dost seek.

*John Greenleaf Whittier,*
*written between 1863 and 1871*

Anger is an index of our discontent that needs to be heeded and carefully channeled. We should find the difficult middle way between uncontrolled anger, which erupts in violence and oppression, and suppressed anger, which may result in silencing individuals to avoid confrontations, ultimately amounting to a greater violence to all involved.

*Baltimore Yearly Meeting, 1988*

Anxiety about showing our negative feelings is such, however, that we often botch the job even when we do try to speak directly to another person. A common occurrence is that we wait until the other has clearly made some mistake, transgressed a rule or convention or agreement for which we can hold them accountable, and then we show them our righteous anger. But the feelings we show tend to be out of proportion to the occasion, because we fail to mention all the other ways in which they have made us angry long before the incident.

*J. Diedrick Snoek, 1973*

~ The first skill [of conflict resolution] is *naming*: being clear and honest about the problem as I see it, stating what I see and how I feel about it. What is important about these statements is that I own them: "I see," "I feel." . . .

~ The second skill is the skill of *listening*: Listening not just to the words, but to the feelings and needs behind the words . . . ; being truly open to what we're hearing (even if it hurts); being open to the possibility that we might ourselves be changed by what we hear.

~ The third skill is the skill of *letting go*: I don't mean that in the sense of giving up, lying down and inviting people to walk all over us, but acknowledging the possibility that there may be other solutions to this conflict than the ones we've thought of yet; letting the imagination in—making room for the Spirit. We need to let go of our own will—not so as to surrender to another's, but so as to look together for God's solution. If we are to do any of these things well—naming, listening, letting go—we need to have learned to trust that of God in ourselves and that of God in those trapped on all sides of the conflict with us.

*Mary Lou Leavitt, 1986*

When I seek truth, right, or communion rather than victory, my adversary is precisely the teacher I need. . . . My own position's greatest truth-deficiency must be corrected with the truth to be found in my adversary's position. As I correct my position's deficiencies, it becomes more coherent and more nearly complete, requiring a new response from its adversaries, which in turn may yield further gleanings for still another position.

*Jim Corbett, 1991*

I have heard some Friends deny their anger in a silent "peace" where there is no understanding of each other. . . . How do we become reconciled to each other if we are asunder? All I can say is to go up to that person and say what is in your heart; that their ways are hurting you but you still love them. But this takes time and not many people like to look in a person's face and find out who they are. So we miss the reconciliation and do not have the experience—that we cared. Given that, then we will know who we are and find relief in tears we all should share. This is where peace starts.

*Sue Norris, 1982*

QUERIES

 ❧ *During conflict, do I adhere to the discipline of speaking truth in love?*

 ❧ *When involved in disputes, do I seek truth and reconciliation rather than victory?*

 ❧ *Do I seek to hear the causes of misunderstanding, fear, or defensiveness in others, and do I try to share something of myself that may help explain my anxiety and fear around an issue?*

The Community of God shall be built
by those who can suffer and forgive and love,
and overcome evil with good.

*Emil Fuchs, 1949*

Forgiving is essential in a community of hurt and hurtful persons. There is, however, such a cultural confusion about what constitutes forgiveness. . . .

~ First, we tend to confuse forgiveness with a spirit of indifference, the pretense that it does not matter. "Oh, that is all right; it really did not hurt me anyway!" That is not forgiving; it is lying. The truth is that these things matter a great deal and it does not help to avoid the issue.

~ Second, there is the mistaken idea that to forgive is to cease from hurting. . . . It is simply not true that the act of forgiving necessarily erases the hurt. Hurting is not evil. We may hurt for a long time to come.

~ Third, many would have us believe that in order to forgive we must forget. But this is not the case. To erase the memory would do violence to the human personality.

~ Fourth, we trick ourselves into believing that to forgive means that the relationship can be just the same as before the offense. We might as well make peace with the fact that the relationship will never be the same again. By the grace of God, it can be a hundred times better, but it will never be the same. We destroy ourselves and all those around us when we pretend that things are just the same as before.

*Richard J. Foster, 1987*

. . . Few of us will believe in and accept the forgiveness of God so completely as to let God bury our sin in forgiving mercy; or who, having once accepted God's forgiveness, will leave our sin with God forever. We are always re-opening the vault where we have deposited our sin, and are forever asking to have it back in order to fondle it, to reconstruct, to query, to worry over it, to wear it inwardly. Thus our sin ties us to the past, and finally dooms our lives . . . in the present and the future.

*Douglas Steere, 1962*

You may hear someone say, "She forgave him, but he can't forgive himself." But I wonder if we can ever forgive ourselves? We have an accuser inside us who speaks with a voice not ours: whether it is the Freudian superego, the social conscience, or God, or the devil. (The word "devil" means accuser. . . .) When the voice of this accuser falls silent, we feel at peace. But we cannot still it ourselves—and the cost of deafening ourselves to it is too high. And yet the teaching of the gospels is that God's forgiveness is always there, waiting for us. We can accept it, though we can do nothing to earn it; but we can only receive it if we are willing to let it change us.

Forgiveness, human and divine, looks forward. It is the means whereby the future can be different from the past. It is not the same as resignation or acceptance because of this element of hope; it believes that things can change. This means that there is no forgiveness except when we are willing ourselves to change.

*John Lampen, 1987*

[They say] "Forgive and forget.". . . [But] forgiveness has nothing to do with forgetting, and forgetting certainly has nothing to do with forgiveness.

In fact, the power of forgiveness is in the letting go of something "owed," usually to oneself or to another, according to my etymological dictionary. In forgiving, I am neither approving or condemning, I am simply releasing a demand for tribute, or payment for a past transgression. Actually my resentments seem to be demands. I tend to fondle and stroke the hurts, real or imagined, from the past and to continue to demand that tribute be paid to me because of their having happened. And the paying of the tribute, someone's contrition, usually does not satisfy, since the hunger or craving for more persists. If I can forgive, that is to say, to release my demand for tribute, then I am the one who is freed from the hunger or craving for payment.

*Tom Hoskins, 1993*

The best definition I've ever heard for forgiveness is giving up the
right to hurt someone for the hurt they've done to you.

*Joyce Sams, 1994*


Relationships can heal
but experiences cannot be erased.

*Zachary Hunter, 1991*


"Must I restore what I have not stolen?"

Psalm 69.4 (Jewish Publication Society)

. . . I became aware of my belief that I could only heal if others
admitted their fault and affirmed the reality of what had been
done to me. Like the psalmist I cried, "In the day of my trouble
I seek the Lord . . . my soul refuses to be comforted" (77.2). I realized I was crying out to God while refusing to open myself to
God's healing. I was giving over to others the power to heal,
which belongs only to God, and in so doing was allowing the life
in me to be buried. I repented of my lack of faith, and God began
working in me. . . .

From this experience I know that our healing is not dependent on having the ones who hurt us take responsibility for what
they did and for its effect on us. If this were true, I could never
be whole. . . . There comes a time when it does not matter who
did what and when—or what was stolen. The question is: What
restores life now? Yes, we must restore what we have not stolen—
for the life of all.

*Janet Hoffman, 1996*


When William Blake raised the question as to whether there were
anything absolutely new in the teaching of Jesus of Nazareth, he
responded to his own query: "Only one thing, the importance
Jesus attached to forgiveness." . . . Is this not what we would
expect in one of the most highly evolved persons ever to grace
this planet? How many times should we forgive the offending
brother or sister? "I say unto you not seven times but seventy

times seven." That is to say, never stop forgiving! And this applies to oneself as well.

*John Yungblut, 1994*


We are called upon to love the loveless and the unlovable, to reach out to the racists and the torturers, to all who hurt and damage, cripple and kill. They are God's unhappy children who need especial care. They have harmed themselves, but not irredeemably; and God, through us, and in many other ways, offers them healing love and divine pity and takes their hurts away.

We are called to that obedience which freely gives up self, possessions, life, beliefs, in following that vision, that greater love in which alone is life and peace. This does not mean that we lie down like doormats to be trampled on, or that we give up our freedom or our grasp of truth—it means that we join ourselves to the risk of creation, to the venture of authentic human being, that we "stand in the Light," reveal that measure of truth that is known to us . . . that we face the pain of the world and match it with forgiveness.

*Janet Scott, 1980*


By your capacity for forgiveness shall I recognize your God. . . .

*Marius Grout, 1945*


It is a severe rebuke upon us
That God makes us so many allowances
And we make so few to our neighbor. . . .

*William Penn, 1682*


When two persons want reconciliation through forgiveness, the whole cosmos is involved, and the energy springing from forgiveness is released for other forms of service. Forgiveness makes possible a deeper communion than that which existed before. One can begin to see another reason why forgiveness is important. Its importance is on the scale of evolution and it springs from the Creator of evolution. It invariably releases love, and love is the energy of creation.

*John Yungblut, 1994*

QUERIES

❧ *How does my unwillingness to accept God's forgiveness keep me tied to the past?*

❧ *Do I accept that my forgiveness and healing cannot be dependent on others taking responsibility for their harmful actions or apologizing to me?*

❧ *Do I endeavor to face the pain of the world and match it with forgiveness?*

# CHAPTER 8

Let Us See What Love Can Do in

Practicing Nonviolence

Seeking Equality for All

Listening to the Earth

Spirit-Led Service

A gang of roving bandits who terrorized the backcountry of North Carolina in the mid-1700s captured seventeen-year-old Joseph Cook and threatened to murder him if he did not join their band. After Joseph explained that he was a Quaker and that his conscience would not allow him to kill another person, the ruffians began making plans to shoot him. While they were discussing his execution, Mary Herbert, a young Quaker woman about Joseph's age, suddenly appeared in their midst. She demanded that they let Joseph go and boldly stated that they could not have him because Joseph belonged to her. When the startled bandits refused her, she surprised them by grabbing Joseph and carrying him away in her arms. The captain of the bandits, presumably amused and certain that she could not carry him very far, shouted after her, "When you put him down we will start shooting." Mary, empowered by love, found the strength to carry Joseph well beyond the range of their guns. Quaker journals from that period reveal that "two years later Mary established a legal claim to Joseph by marrying him."[16]

There is love locked in our hearts waiting to empower us with strength beyond our imagining. The power to overcome evil by witnessing to love lies within us all, waiting to be released. Yet most of us keep this transforming power locked away, and we die having never dared to use it.

Now is the time to listen within and unlock the transforming power of our love. If we dare to listen deeply, we hear love calling, inviting us to plain living, to "do no harm," and to respect, love, and serve one another. Hope is whispering to us from the future, calling us each by name, beseeching us to open our hearts because only then will the world be transformed by what Love is waiting to do.

Peace begins within ourselves.
It is to be implemented
within the family, in our meetings,
in our work and leisure,
in our own localities, and internationally.
The task will never be done.
Peace is a process to engage in,
not a goal to be reached.

*Sydney Bailey, 1993*


There is no way to peace,
Peace is the way.

*Lawrence S. Apsey, in 1991, remembers A. J.
Muste attributing these words to Emily Greene
Balch (1867-1961)*


. . . While loving one's enemies does not necessarily mean liking them or even approving of them, it always means treating them as fellow human beings and not denying their humanity. . . . There is nothing in the life of Christ which says one cannot have opponents and even persecutors, but one cannot really have enemies, people whose lives and welfare have a negative value for you.

*Kenneth E. Boulding, 1986*


I would like to suggest a new word to replace enemy. The word is "stranger." It's a very old word, and a good one. We have no more enemies, but we have strangers. Sometimes we are estranged from ourselves and from God. When we meet a person we call a stranger, that person has to be listened to. . . . There is no tribal group to my knowledge that does not have a tradition for dealing with the stranger.

That is, when a person you have no way of labeling or categorizing appears on the horizon, that person is defined as a stranger. An emissary is sent out to question the stranger until some basis for relationship has been found. When, through lengthy discussion, that basis has been found, the stranger is brought to the community and introduced: "Here is so-and-so, and this is how we are connected to her." Now the former stranger has an identity. This process of dialoguing with a person to find a basis for relationship, not agreement or consensus but simply a basis for relationship, is a widely practiced ritual in many parts of the world. Oddly enough, we have lost it in industrial society. Therefore we have enemies. We don't have rituals for deciding the basis of relationships.

*Elise Boulding, 1975*

We are a people that follow after those things that make for peace, love, and unity; it is our desire that others' feet may walk in the same. We do deny and bear our testimony against all strife and wars and contentions. Our weapons are not carnal, but spiritual. Treason, treachery, and false dealings we do utterly deny, and speak the Truth in plainness and singleness of heart.

*Margaret Fell, 1660*

. . . When we are confronted with hurt to ourselves or others, and the rational ways of mending it are not effective, we are forced to choose between complicity in the universal wrong and an act of sacrifice. Then the divine voice inside us insists that this is the most important choice of all. . . .

The journey, the renunciation, the heroism, may be called for within our own hearts, a private matter between us and God. It happens when we accept the hurt, and do not let it enslave or degrade us, but endure it, and refuse to pass it on. When we choose this path, we cannot foresee its end; we can't say if it will do any good. It is a starting point, not a solution. We don't know what will be asked of us next. But by this sacrifice we have identified ourselves with whatever power there is in the universe to redeem and recreate. . . .

*John Lampen, 1987*

The issue [pacifism] came to focus when I was trying to determine whether I could call myself a conscientious objector, recognizing that such a step would mean forswearing violence for the rest of my life. . . . This long period of constant worry culminated in one sleepless night which I spent arguing with myself, going over the arguments of others, praying for guidance and being afraid that I might have my prayers answered. Finally, early in the morning, I knew I had crossed a line. No new arguments fell into place, nothing became more rational, but somewhere I had changed and I knew that I would have to declare myself a conscientious objector. . . .

When I acknowledged that the commitment had been made, I did not feel any inner peace. I knew my decision would cut me off from some members of my family and might even require that I go to prison. I also knew that I had been led inevitably to this choice, but I felt frightened at what had happened to me. Suddenly I was utterly defenseless in a violent world, and for a long time I went through my days fearful of what it meant to have disarmed myself. Since then, there have been a number of times that I have been in some real or potential danger—at peace actions, working in the ghetto, or confronting irrational or violent people. In those times I have not been without fear, but I have never since felt the fear I felt when I first made the commitment to give up reliance on violence to protect me. I believe that when I became convinced of the peace testimony, I was given a leading which, in effect, immersed me in the terror and stuff of violence so that I could know my condition and work with it. I was tested and strengthened in conditions of safety before I was ever tested in real conflict.

*Paul A. Lacey, 1985*


Let us then try what love will do,
for if people did once see we love them
we should soon find they would not harm us.
Force may subdue, but love gains.

*William Penn, 1693*

We tend to rise to what is expected of us. No human being is so depraved that nothing but force can appeal to them. There are many extraordinary instances in Quaker history in which an evil-doer has been suddenly halted and transformed by the power of nonresistance combined with good will.

*Howard Brinton, 1966*

On more than one occasion the places where anti-slavery meetings were held were attacked by mobs. These angry crowds threw things through the windows, shouted out, and beat on the doors. They waited outside to abuse the people when they came out. Once in New York, Lucretia Mott was being escorted out of a meeting hall by a gentleman. When she saw how the ruffians were handling the persons who had spoken, she insisted on her friend going to help some of the more timid women. He of course didn't want to leave her and said, "But how will you get through?" She laid her hand on the arm of one of the roughest men in the crowd and replied, "This man will see me through." And he did.

*Shirley Spain, 1943*

In 1967, several hundred Friends from New York Yearly Meeting came together for an Easter Sunday pilgrimage to carry money and boxes of medical supplies labeled for both North and South Vietnam across the Peace Bridge into Canada. . . .

Easter Sunday dawned and Friends gathered for a powerful meeting for worship "with a sense of . . . the leading of God's hand in what we were doing." At the bridge the group was confronted by a representative of the U.S. Bureau of Foreign Assets Control, who warned all who stepped onto the bridge that they might be arrested, charged with trading with the enemy, and given ten years in prison and $10,000 fines. Many were aware they had never before stood so strongly and clearly for what they believed. Friends walked without incident as far as the Canadian Entry of Customs, where a customs official informed them that Canada was not authorized at that time to receive any parcels bound for Vietnam. Feeling that they had no recourse but to wait and see where they might be led, the group settled into a silent meeting for worship. They had not been there long when they heard a phone ring in another room followed by excited discussion. The customs official reappeared to inform them that the Canadian government had changed its policy.

*Hugh Barbour, et al., 1995*

We must start with our own hearts and minds.
Wars will stop only when each of us is convinced
that war is never the way. . . .

We must relinquish the desire to own other people,
to have power over them, and
to force our views on to them.
We must own up to our own negative side
and not look for scapegoats
to blame, punish, or exclude.
We must resist the urge towards waste and
the accumulation of possessions.

In speaking out, we acknowledge that we
ourselves, are as limited and as erring as anyone else.
When put to the test, we each may fall short.
Together let us reject the clamor of fear
And listen to the whisperings of hope.

*New Zealand Yearly Meeting, 1987*

QUERIES

☙ How am I practicing nonviolence within myself, my family, and my community?

☙ Do I treat wrongdoers in loving ways that allow them to rise above their wrongdoing?

☙ Am I willing to accept and endure hurt both without passing it on and without letting it degrade me?

. . . The divine Light
is accessible to all people,
regardless of race, sex,
age, or material wealth.
Everyone has the potential
to respond to God within. . . .
Equality is not sameness.
It is equality of respect.
Every person is a child of God.

*New England Yearly Meeting, 1985*

Paul Cuffe was the son of a freed slave and an Indian woman of the Wampanaog tribe. He became a Quaker and was the captain of a prosperous fleet of large boats crewed by black sailors.

In 1780 Paul and his brother John petitioned the General Court of Massachusetts for relief from taxation saying they had "no vote or influence in the election of those that tax us." The Cuffes then were imprisoned for non-payment of their taxes. Eventually they were released and their taxes were reduced. As a result of their act of conscience, within three years, the state passed a law which gave blacks full legal and voting rights.

*Based on information from Daisy Newman, 1972*

All of us are enmeshed in that net of racism, whether we choose to be or not. But there is hope. Let me share an analogy with you. . . . Racism is very much like alcoholism. The alcoholic doesn't choose or intend to be an alcoholic; neither you nor I choose or intend to be racists, or to benefit from a racist society. Both are things that happen to us, through no choice of our own, without our intent. The alcoholic is not a wicked, evil person; neither are you and I. . . . The illness of racism, like alcoholism, is not my fault; but it is my responsibility. I didn't cause it, but I must and can control it.

In both cases—racism and alcoholism—the first step on the road to health is to acknowledge the reality, to stop making excuses, to stop denying it. We need to face the facts before we can cope with them. In both cases you're never fully cured; the alcoholic is always an alcoholic. And I really doubt, sadly, that those of us who grew up in a racist society can ever totally shed our uncon-scious racist attitudes. But we can take responsibility for our actions from now on. . . . We can choose to work to end racism, and learn skills to do that.

*Alison D. Oldham, 1984*


As male and female are made one in Jesus Christ,
so women receive an office in the truth as well as men. . . .

*Elizabeth Bathurst, 1685*


Friends interpreted the success of women as ministers and lead-ers [in the 1600s] as evidence that God was restoring creation to its state of original wholeness. The persecutions and sufferings of women ministers were seen as evidence of the continued wicked-ness of the world, the government, and the established church, and the need for redemption.

*Mary Garmon, 1996*


When [Susan B.] Anthony was once asked, "Do you pray?" she responded, "I pray every second of my life; not on my knees, but with my work. My prayer is to lift women to equality with men. Work and worship are one with me."

*Hugh Barbour, et al., 1995*


In 1976, I [said] . . . that if we [the United States] were to survive for two hundred more years, we would need the contributions of those left out of the Declaration of Independence: people of color, Native Americans, women, the poor, children and young people. I said:

~   that we must internalize that the majority of the world's pop-ulation is dark-skinned, and our arrogant assumption of white superiority is no longer endurable;

~ that indigenous people can point the way to a simpler lifestyle and a less destructive world-view;

~ that women can help us make decisions at a national level, as well as a personal level, on the basis of caring about people and about the earth, rather than on the basis of greed and self-interest;

~ that homeless and hungry and unemployed people make a mockery of our boast of "liberty and justice for all";

~ that children need a future in which to live and dream and make their contributions to the world.

*Elizabeth Watson, 1992*

QUERIES

℔ Do I look for and recognize that of God in all people?

℔ How do I monitor and change the deep-seated prejudices I have acquired from my family, church, community, and culture?

℔ Am I committed to learning the skills necessary to end racism and other forms of prejudice and discrimination?

It would go a great way to caution and direct people in their use of the world if we were better studied and knowledgeable about the creation of it. For how could we find the confidence to abuse it, while we should see the Great Creator stare us in the face, in all and every part thereof?

*William Penn, 1692*

. . . I think that each of us will be fully human only when we recognize the full Alive-ness of all Creation, and act on that recognition, when we learn to "speak to that of God in Everything," and to humbly admit our dependence upon that great Web we call Creation. Hear the words of Old Jack, an elderly farmer in one of Wendell Berry's novels:

. . . We are members of each other. All of us. Everything. The difference ain't in who is a member and who is not, but in who knows it and who don't.

*Lisa Lofland Gould, 1999*

Through the lens of the Spirit I can see, though imperfectly, that we are all one in creation. . . . In the deepest sense, my individuality is an illusion.

*Bruce Birchard, 1997*

To be at home in wildlands, one must accept and share life as a gift that is unearned and unowned. When we cease to work at taming the Creation and learn to accept life as a gift, a way opens for us to become active participants in an ancient exodus out of idolatry and bondage—a pilgrimage that continues to be conceived and born in wilderness.

*Jim Corbett, 1991*

You don't have to hurry. You can stroll or you can saunter. "Saunter" comes from "Sainte Terre," meaning "The Holy

Land." Walk as if you were sauntering to the Holy Land, trusting the land beneath your feet to be holy—now—here!

Teresina Havens, 1992

"The press of my foot to the earth springs a hundred affections,"
wrote Walt Whitman. If I am in need of affection I take a walk.
Trails surfaced with grass or wood chips are kind to the feet and
to the earth beneath. In a desert landscape, patterned sand and
gravel carpet the walkways. If I have affection to spare, I can
imprint the earth beneath my feet with joy.

Francis D. Hole, 1994

Sometimes it is suggested that we interpret "domination" to
mean "stewardship." We should assume a responsible, caretaking
role of the other species. But stewardship and caretaking still
imply unequal status. The steward presumes to know best what is
good for those cared for and does not necessarily consult with
them about what they want or think they need or how they feel.

One of the prices we have paid for civilization is the loss of a
relationship of mutuality with animals. Joan McIntyre, editor of
. . . Mind in the Water, says: "Animals were once, for all of us,
teachers. They instructed us in ways of being and perceiving that
extended our imaginations and that were models for additional
possibilities. We watched them make their way through the intri-
cacies of their lives with wonder and awe."

Elizabeth Watson, 1991

As long as gold and stocks are seen as the necessary capital to sus-
tain life, communities will be compelled to convert whole forests
to cash and entire mountainsides to bonds. Sustainability
requires that a community feel itself linked to the land and to
those who will live there after its members. They must grasp the
essential truth that the capital upon which their life and all life
depends is the living infrastructure of the planet. If they do, they
will fashion an economic system with the discipline and wisdom
to invest for the long term. . . . They would think about "the

seventh generation" and . . . in the face of absolute ignorance they would be conservative, knowing that they would "never know more than a small part of what [they] need to know."

*Ted Bernard and Jora Young, 1997*

Have you heard cries from Rwanda, as Hutu and Tutsi battle one another? Surely we have all grieved over the senseless deaths in these and so many places where human madness has won out over human kindness. Can you then not hear the sound of ecosystems dying, the cry of thousands of species looking for members of their communities, which are no longer? . . .

That there are mourners there is no question. The grief comes tentatively, personally, "Where is the indigo bunting I used to see on the telephone wires every summer over by the Johnson farm?" "Did you hear a whippoorwill this summer? We never heard one at our place." "I haven't seen a luna moth in years." And there are other questions, bravely framed as scientific inquiry, but secretly as laments: "Have you noticed there seem to be far fewer shells on the beaches?" "Are the number of snakes declining in the state?" "Doesn't it seem to you that there are fewer insects?"

I believe the need to mourn what's being lost is crucial. The loss of a warbler song in May, or the destruction of a favorite meadow, are personal losses. The grief is essential, and to deny it is to keep a wound festering. But society at large does not recognize the dying, and therefore rejects the need to mourn, under the guise that the mourner is merely lamenting "progress." And the grief is deepened, I think, knowing we are both mourner and murderer, the bereaved as well as the executioner. "I am become Death," were Oppenheimer's words, I believe, when he witnessed the first atomic bomb explosion. Does it not feel at times that we "are become death," our culture and our diseased ways?

*Lisa Lofland Gould, 1999*

We seem to be at a turning point in human history. We can choose life or watch the planet become uninhabitable for our species. Somehow, I believe that we will pass through this dark night of our planetary soul to a new period of harmony with the God that is to be found within each of us, and that S/He will inspire renewed confidence in people everywhere, empowering us all to cooperate, to use our skills, our wisdom, our creativity, our love, our faith—even our doubts and fears—to make peace with the planet. Strengthened by this fragile faith, empowered by the Spirit within, I dare to hope.

*Pat Sauders, 1987*

. . . I have not come half way across the continent to tell you there is no hope. I do believe it possible that we may make the drastic changes needed to save Earth for human habitation. . . . I believe that we will do it, because we cannot look our children in the eye if we do not try. . . . O deep in my heart, I do believe we shall overcome, but "some day" may be too late. George Fox said, "Ye have no time but this present."

*Elizabeth Watson, 1992*

QUERIES

- Do I look for and see the face of God in all creation?

- Do I spend time in wild places listening for what I might learn?

- Have I mourned the loss of species and the harm done by pollution, and am I aware of my part in these losses? Do I endeavor to change my personal as well as societal practices as an expression of hope for the future?

True godliness does not
turn people out of the world,
but enables them to live better in it,
and excites their endeavors to mend it;
not hide their candle under a bushel,
but to set it upon a table in a candlestick.

*William Penn, 1682*


We shall find them [opportunities for service] among our neighbors as well as among strangers, in our own families as well as in unfamiliar circles—magnificent opportunities to be kind and patient and understanding.

This is a vocation just as truly as some more obviously seen as such—the vocation of ordinary men and women called to continual unspectacular acts of loving kindness in the ordinary setting of everyday. They need no special medical boards before they embark on their service, need no inoculation against anything but indifference and lethargy and perhaps a self-indulgent shyness. How simple it sounds; how difficult it often is; how possible it may become by the grace of God.

*Clifford Haigh, 1962*


The need is for being rather than doing, in the knowledge that action will take care of itself if an energy of goodness, justice, and peace is encouraged to flow. This means not so much being good—as allowing good to be in you. . . .

*Damaris Parker-Rhodes, 1985*


In all our fervor—
in all my fervor—to be doing,
have I paid too little attention
to the power that lies in being?
Do we remember that it is the spirit of our service,
the aura that surrounds it,

the gentleness and the patience
that marks it,
the love made visible
that compels it,
that is the truly distinctive quality . . . ?

*Stephen G. Cary, 1979*

As long as there is inward chaos, all outward actions will be con-
taminated by this chaos. In such a case all that we do will promote
rather than allay confusion. We seek to bring peace in the world
when there is no peace in our hearts, and as a result we infect the
outer world with our inner conflict. As an old Chinese saying has
it, "The right action performed by the wrong man is the wrong
action."

*Howard Brinton, 1948*

My heart is beating fast.
Landing,
there is the smell of heat;
beggars enclose me.
They don't say a word, but
their eyes are screaming,
"Help me, help me!"

I am ten years old;
I want to help them but
I can't.
I don't say a word,
but with my eyes I say,
"I'm coming,
I'm coming."

*Mira McClelland, 1998*

I expect to pass through this world but once; any good thing
therefore that I can do, or any kindness that I can show to any

fellow creature, let me do it now; let me not defer or neglect it, for I shall not pass this way again.

*Stephen Grellet, 1800*


John and Diana Lampen . . . have worked for many years in Northern Ireland. I heard them speak about recent break-throughs there. . . . After all these years, it is impossible to say what changed and why. The Lampens used the image of a vast accumulation of feathers. One day, one more feather, one more hopelessly insignificant act, finally shifts the balance of the scales. The peace process proceeds slowly and ambivalently. But it has gotten this far by the accumulation of many personal efforts and individual transformations. May God continue to pour feathers on Northern Ireland and on all of us!

*Doug Gwyn, 1996*


And that is why such small undertakings as we make are impor-tant—far beyond their actual dimensions. They have an aura of the infinite about their heads. Viewed in the small, these under-takings are minute, against the world's sufferings, these little ges-tures of behavior and acted concern. But they are acted symbols, media of communication of the life of the Spirit . . . and spoken to the world.

*Thomas R. Kelly, 1938*


In Spanish the verb "esperar" means both to hope and to wait. From a faith perspective, hoping and waiting are related in a pos-itive, expectant way. Hopeful waiting is to expect grace, to believe that God promises, as Fox affirmed, that an ocean of light will ultimately overcome an ocean of darkness. In English the verb "to wait" means both to be expectant and to serve. Hoping, wait-ing, and serving are basic elements to the good and faithful life.

*Tom Ewell, 1999*

Those who go forth
ministering to the wants and necessities
of their fellow human beings,
experience a rich return,
their souls being as a watered garden,
as a spring that faileth not.

*Lucretia Mott, 1850*

QUERIES

  ❧ *Do I seek opportunities to both provide loving care for my family and do service in my community?*

  ❧ *Do I remember that it is the spirit of my service that makes love visible?*

  ❧ *Am I faithfully serving God by seeking justice and showing loving kindness to all I meet?*

# APPENDIX

Glossary of Common Quaker Terms

Biographical Information

Notes

Acknowledgments

*These definitions are based on glossaries from the* Faith and Practice *or* Book of Discipline *from Mid-America, Ohio Valley, Philadelphia, and North Pacific Yearly Meetings of the Religious Society of Friends, and from Janet Hoffman's Testimonies List.*

**The AFSC** (American Friends Service Committee) is the Quaker service and relief organization that was awarded the Nobel Peace Prize in 1947 for its restoration work in post-war Europe.

**Birthright Friend** is a Quaker born of parents who were members of the Religious Society of Friends at the time of the person's birth.

**Centering** is a spiritual effort to focus our hearts and minds to listen for how God may be speaking to us.

**Clearness Committee** consists of people appointed by the meeting to help an individual or group explore whether their decisions and plans are aligned with God's will for them.

**The Clerk** is a servant-leader entrusted with facilitating a Friends Meeting for Business. The dynamic between the clerk and the meeting is that the clerk draws out, discerns, and articulates the meeting's understanding of truth during the Meeting for Business.

**Continuing Revelation** is the belief that God continues to speak to people today.

**Discernment** is the individual or group spiritual practice of coming to know God's will by prayerfully sifting through what we have heard while listening within, and recognizing and separating it from our own frailties such as fear, pride, and ambition.

***Faith and Practice*** is the name given to a book of reference compiled by each yearly meeting that contains the collective wisdom of the community including queries and guidelines intended to support individual and corporate faithful living.

**Gathered Meetings** are those times in worship when there is a heightened sense of the presence of God among the worshipers.

**Inner Light** is the presence of God in our hearts which illuminates truth and strengthens and guides us. It is sometimes referred to by Friends as the Spirit, the Guide, the Holy, the Spirit of Truth, the Inward Christ, and "that of God in everyone."

**Leading** is an inner sense that God is calling us to undertake a particular course of action.

**Meeting for Business** is a meeting for worship during which the business decisions of the community are made by corporate discernment.

**Meetings for Worship** in the tradition of "unprogrammed meetings" are worship services where Friends gather in expectant silence, waiting upon God and the leadings of the Spirit, which may manifest in vocal messages, prayer, or silent communion. These services are not led by a pastor and do not have a pre-arranged program. In the tradition of "programmed" Quaker meetings, there is also the spirit of expectant waiting, but the worship is led by a pastor and there is an established order of service.

**Monthly, Quarterly, and Yearly Meetings** constitute the institutional structure of Friends which is organized geographically by a calendar nomenclature (monthly, quarterly, yearly) designating the regularity of their business meetings. Local Quaker meetings are called "monthly meetings" because they meet monthly to conduct business. Quarterly meetings consist of several regional monthly meetings which typically meet every three months. Yearly meetings are made up of several quarterly meetings, often within a state or nation, which meet together once a year.

**Proceed as Way Opens** is a phrase referring to Friends' practice of waiting for divine guidance, and then moving forward with the faith that God's will and direction will continue to be revealed.

**Quaker** (interchangeable with Friend) is the traditional or popular name of a member of the Religious Society of Friends. It was originally a derogatory term given by the Puritans to early Friends who sometimes "quaked" during worship or when giving public testimony.

**Queries** are reflection questions, usually based on Friends' testimonies, which are read and pondered for spiritual guidance by individuals and by meetings.

**Sense of the Meeting** is the collective understanding or unity of a meeting that is articulated by the clerk for approval by the meeting.

**Testimonies** are outward practices, reflective of Friends' inward faith. Traditional Friends' testimonies include simplicity, peace, integrity, community, and equality.

# Biographical Information
## on the primary authors

**Hugh Barbour** (1921– ) Author of numerous books on Quakerism, lecturer, and Professor of Quaker History at Earlham College of Religion for thirty-eight years.

**Ellen Sophia Bosanquet** (1875–1965) British author, artist, and world traveler who grew up in a Quaker family in Northumberland.

**Elise Boulding** (1920– ) Sociologist and feminist with a commitment to peace studies and peace activism; Professor Emerita of Dartmouth College.

**Howard Brinton** (1884–1973) Educator, author, and co-director of Pendle Hill Retreat Center for many years with his wife Anna; AFSC worker in Germany and Poland.

**John Calvi** (1952– ) Massage therapist, healer, and lecturer who travels widely with a leading to help people heal from trauma.

**Edgar B. Castle** (1898–1973) British educator and interpreter of Quakerism for youth and spiritual seekers; Headmaster at Leighton Park and Professor of Education at Hull, England.

**Jim Corbett** (1933– ) Teacher, writer, goat herder, and co-establisher of the "new underground railroad" for Central American refugees through the U.S.-Mexican borderlands.

**Sandra Cronk** (1942–2000) Spiritual nurturer, writer, teacher, historian of religions, and founding member of School of the Spirit.

**Margaret Fell** (1614–1702) British spiritual leader and tract writer imprisoned three times for religious beliefs, and often credited with the organizational development of the early Friends movement; wife of George Fox.

**Richard J. Foster** (1942– ) Writer, teacher, author of five books, theologian, and founder of RENOVARE, an infra-church movement committed to the renewal of the Church in all her multi-faceted expressions.

**George Fox** (1624–1691) British spiritual leader, who with his wife, Margaret Fell, is credited with the formation of the Religious Society of Friends; author, healer, and preacher who traveled widely in the ministry persevering through religious persecution and frequent imprisonments.

**Janet Hoffman** (1939– ) Educator, writer, lecturer, and workshop leader in North America and abroad on Quaker ways of personal and corporate discernment.

**Rufus M. Jones** (1863–1948) Long-time Professor of Philosophy at Haverford College; a founding member of the AFSC; international lecturer, and prolific writer who authored fifty-four books.

**Thomas R. Kelly** (1893–1941) Professor of Philosophy at Haverford College; spiritual teacher and inspired author of books about the mystical experience.

**Paul A. Lacey** (1934– ) Professor of Literature at Earlham College; active in civil rights and peace activities.

**Diana Lampen** (1940– ) and **John Lampen** (1938– ) British authors who ran a school for emotionally disturbed boys; worked for peace in Northern Ireland, and now teach peacemaking and meditation worldwide.

**Frank Levering** (1952– ) and **Wanda Urbanska** (1956– ) Left successful writing careers in Los Angeles to run a family orchard in Virginia and live simpler lives; worked with PBS on the "Affluenza" special; founded Orchard Gap Press, specializing in books on fruit, simple living, and small-town life.

**Patricia Loring** (1936– ) Spiritual nurturer, author of books on listening spirituality, workshop leader, retreat director, and personal spiritual guide.

**Lucretia Mott** (1793–1880) Abolitionist who helped found the Philadelphia Female Antislavery Society; feminist and one of the primary organizers of the conference on women's rights at Seneca Falls.

**Carol R. Murphy** (1916– ) Writer of numerous pamphlets on spirituality; life-long spiritual seeker; active in Friends' publications.

**Daisy Newman** (1904–1994) Best-selling novelist whose books provide a popular interpretation of Quaker customs and values.

**Parker J. Palmer** (1939– ) Widely-read contemporary author on education and spiritual development, teacher, and activist; senior associate of the American Association for Higher Education and senior adviser to the Fetzer Institute.

**Damaris Parker-Rhodes** (1918–1986) British peace activist who was active in Labour politics and ecumenical activities; writer, lecturer, and workshop leader.

**Sharon Daloz Parks** (1942– ) Former Professor at Harvard Divinity School and consultant to the Harvard Business and Kennedy Schools; lecturer and widely-read author in faith development and the pursuit of the civic "commons"; presently a Fellow at the Whidbey Institute.

**Isaac Penington** (1616–1679) British spiritual seeker who wrote several volumes on Quaker religious experience, and who was persecuted and imprisoned by the Puritans for his religious beliefs.

**William Penn** (1644–1718) British writer and founder of the state of Pennsylvania; wrote a Frame of Government for the colony that served as a model for the U.S. Constitution.

**John Punshon** (1935– ) Former British solicitor and borough councillor in Leyton; author and Professor of Quaker Studies at Earlham School of Religion.

**Barbara Cummings St. John** (1914– ) Birthright Friend, writer, and spiritual nurturer among New England Quakers.

**Emily Sander** (1931– ) Birthright Friend, social worker, watercolorist, and spiritual nurturer among New England Quakers.

**Hannah Whitall Smith** (1832–1911) Victorian author and lecturer; part of the Holiness revivalist movement.

**Douglas Steere** (1901–1997) Prolific writer on prayer and the spiritual life; long-time Professor of Philosophy at Haverford College; traveled worldwide on behalf of the AFSC.

**Elizabeth Gray Vining** (1902–2000) Educator and author of children's books, essays on spirituality, and Quaker biographies; personal tutor for Crown Prince Akihito of Japan.

**Elizabeth Watson** (1914– ) Feminist and spiritual writer; lecturer and workshop leader with a life-long commitment to equality, social justice, and environmental sustainability.

**John Greenleaf Whittier** (1807–1892) Internationally known poet; national leader in the abolitionist movement, and writer of anti-slavery tracts.

**John Woolman** (1720–1772) Tailor and journalist best known for his successful travels to witness nonviolently against slavery, to protect the rights of Native Americans, and to recognize the relationship between exploitive economic production and the seeds of war and injustice.

**John Yungblut** (1913–1995) Teacher, writer, Jungian scholar, faculty member at Pendle Hill, and Director of the Guild for Spiritual Guidance.

1. Parker J. Palmer, *Let Your Life Speak: Listening for the Voice of Vocation* (San Francisco, CA: Jossey-Bass, 2000), p. 3.

2. T. Canby Jones, "Thomas Kelly as I Remember Him," Pendle Hill Pamphlet 284 (Wallingford, PA: Pendle Hill Publications, 1988), p. 14.

3. Patricia Loring, *Listening Spirituality: Volume I, Personal Spiritual Practices Among Friends* (Washington, DC: Openings Press, 1997), p. 130.

4. John Wilhelm Rowntree, "Man's Relations to God," *Essays and Addresses* (England, 1905), pp. 397-405. *Christian Faith and Practice in the Experience of the Society of Friends* (London Yearly Meeting of the Religious Society of Friends, 1960), #94.

5. Thomas R. Kelly, *A Testament of Devotion* (New York: Harper & Row, 1939), pp. 59-61.

6. Rufus Jones, "Selections from 'The Writings of Rufus M. Jones,'" *Quaker Spirituality: Selected Writings*, Douglas Steere, ed. (Mahwah, NJ: Paulist Press, 1984), p. 282.

7. Henry J. Cadbury, "The Character of a Quaker," Pendle Hill Pamphlet 103 (Lebanon, PA: Sowers, 1959), p. 9. Originally given as the William Penn Lecture for 1959, published by special arrangement with the Young Friends Movement, Philadelphia Yearly Meeting, Philadelphia, PA.

8. John Woolman, *The Journal of John Woolman and a Plea for the Poor* (Secaucus, NJ: The Citadel Press, 1961), p. 151. Originally printed in 1774.

9. Edward Snyder, *Witness in Washington: Fifty Years of Friendly Persuasion*, second printing (Richmond, IN: Friends United Press, 1994), pp. 194-195.

10. Barbara Cummings St. John, conversation recorded in 1995.

11. Thomas R. Kelly, *A Testament of Devotion*, pp. 97-98.

12. Elizabeth Gray Vining, *Contributions of the Quakers* (Great Britain: F. A. Davis Company, 1939). Reprinted by Pendle Hill, Wallingford, PA, 1939, p. 69.

13. L. Violet Hodgkin, *A Book of Quaker Saints* (London: Friends Home Service Committee, 1917), p. 379. Reprinted, 1972. Originally appeared in *The American Friend*, November 28, 1895.

14. Peter and Carole Fingesten, "Let the Silence Speak for Itself," *Friends Journal* (Philadelphia, PA: September 1, 1987).

15. Emily Sander, conversation recorded in 1993—*Charles Verge, family therapist; *Unknown; *Unknown; *Unknown.

16. Carol and John Stoneburner, eds., *The Influence of Quaker Women on American Society: Biographical Studies (Studies in Women and Religion, Vol. 21)* (Lewiston, NY: Edwin Mellen Press, 1986), p. 164.

Grateful acknowledgment is made to all those who shared their work. Every effort has been made to give proper acknowledgment to authors and copyright holders of the text herein. If any omissions or errors have been made, please notify the publisher who will correct it in future editions. The following acknowledgments are for excerpts over 250 words or poetry.

Excerpts on pages 56, 63, 92, and 94 from *Late Harvest: Memories, Letters and Poems* by Ellen Sophia Bosanquet, Chameleon Press, 1971, reprinted by permission of Katherine Bosanquet Potter and the Bosanquet family.

Excerpts on pages 78 and 116 from *In the Manner of the Lord's Prayer, Volume 2*, by Judith L. Brutz © 1990 by Friends Family Service and reprinted by permission of the author.

Excerpts on pages 41, 134, and 162 from *The Influence of Quaker Women on American Society: Biographical Studies* by Carol and John Stoneburner (eds.) © 1989 by the Edwin Mellen Press and reprinted by permission.

Excerpts on pages 59, 101-102, 107, 126-127, and 128 from *New Studies in Mystical Religion* by Rufus Jones © 1928 by the Macmillan Company and reprinted by permission of the Estate of Rufus Jones c/o Mellon Private Asset Management.

Excerpts on pages 89, 171, and 173 from *Caring for Creation: Reflections on the Biblical Basis of Earthcare* by Lisa Lofland Gould © 1999 by Friends Committee on Unity With Nature and reprinted by permission.

Excerpts on pages 35-36, 93, and 172 from *Healing Ourselves and Our Earth* by Elizabeth Watson © 1991 by Friends Committee on Unity With Nature and reprinted by permission.

Excerpt on page 122 from *A Book of Quaker Saints* by L. Violet Hodgkin © 1917 by Friends Home Service Committee and reprinted by permission.

Excerpts from the following Pendle Hill Pamphlets are reprinted by permission of Pendle Hill Publications (Wallingford, PA 19086; 1-800-743-3150): Rose Adede, "Pioneer African Quaker"; Bruce Birchard, "The Burning One-ness Binding Everything: A Spiritual Journey"; Elise Boulding, "Children and Solitude"; Kenneth Boulding, "Mending the World"; Howard Brinton, "The Quaker Doctrine of Inward Peace"; Henry Cadbury, "The Character of a Quaker"; Wilmer Cooper, "The Testimony of Integrity"; Sandra Cronk, "Peace Be with You"; Sandra Cronk, "Gospel Order"; Emil Fuchs, "Christ in Catastrophe"; Tom and Liz Gates, "Stories from Kenya"; Richard Gregg, "The Value of Voluntary Simplicity"; Teresina Havens, "Mind What Stirs in Your Heart"; T. Canby Jones, "Thomas Kelly as I Remember Him"; Rufus Jones, "Rethinking Quaker Principles"; Mary Hoxie Jones, "Thou Dost Open Up My Life"; Thomas Kelly, "Reality of the Spiritual World"; Patricia Loring, "Discernment"; Carol R. Murphy, "Inward Traveller"; Carol R. Murphy, "The Available Mind"; Francis S. Nicholson, "Quaker Money"; Bradford Smith, "Dear Gift of Life"; Beatrice Saxon Snell, "A Joint and Visible Fellowship"; J. Diedrick Snoek, "A Hunger for Community"; Douglas Steere, "On Being Present Where You Are"; Douglas Steere, "On Befriending Others in Prayer"; Patrick Swayne, "Stewardship of Wealth"; Richard Ullman, "Dilemmas of a Reconciler"; Elizabeth Gray Vining, "A Quest There Is"; John Yungblut, "On Hallowing One's Diminishments"; John Yungblut, "For That Solitary Individual."

Excerpts from the following Pendle Hill books and papers are reprinted by permission of Pendle Hill Publishing: Howard Brinton, *Friends for Three Hundred Years*; Mary Garmon, "Hidden in Plain Sight"; Hannah Whitall Smith, "The Quaker Reader"; Elizabeth Gray Vining, *The World in Tune*; Elizabeth Watson, "New Occasions Teach New Duties. Realignment: Nine Views Among Friends."

Many of the sources included here are from the Haverford College Quaker Collection, Haverford College, Haverford, PA.